CULINARY ESSENTIALS

Lab Manual

JOHNSON & WALES
UNIVERSITY

America's Career University®

Glencoe
McGraw-Hill

New York, New York   Columbus, Ohio   Chicago, Illinois   Peoria, Illinois   Woodland Hills, California

Contributors:

Dr. Bradley J. Ware, Professor, College of Culinary Arts, Johnson & Wales University
John Chiaro, C.E.C., C.C.E., A.A.C., Associate Professor, College of Culinary Arts, Johnson & Wales University
Paul Richter, Culinary Arts Instructor, Sea-Tac Occupational Skills Center, Burien, Washington
Denise Schaefer, Culinary Arts Instructor, Penta Career Center, Perrysburg, Ohio
Pamela Cox, Food Service & Catering Instructor, Larkin High School, Elgin, Illinois

---

Safety Notice

The reader is expressly advised to consider and use all safety precautions described in this textbook or that might also be indicated by undertaking the activities described herein. In addition, common sense should be exercised to help avoid all potential hazards and, in particular, to take relevant safety precautions concerning any known or likely hazards involved in food preparation, or in use of the procedures described in *Culinary Essentials,* such as the risk of knife cuts or burns.

Publisher and Authors assume no responsibility for the activities of the reader or for the subject matter experts who prepared this book. Publisher and Authors make no representation or warranties of any kind, including but not limited to, the warranties of fitness for particular purpose or merchantability, nor for any implied warranties related thereto, or otherwise. Publisher and Authors will not be liable for damages of any type, including any consequential, special or exemplary damages resulting, in whole or in part, from reader's use or reliance upon the information, instructions, warnings or other matter contained in this textbook.

Brand Disclaimer

Publisher does not necessarily recommend or endorse any particular company or brand name product that may be discussed or pictured in this textbook. Brand name products are used because they are readily available, likely to be known to the reader, and their use may aid in the understanding of the text. Publisher recognizes that other brand name or generic products may be substituted and work as well or better than those featured in the textbook.

Glencoe/McGraw-Hill

A Division of The McGraw·Hill Companies

Send all inquiries to:
Glencoe/McGraw-Hill
3008 W. Willow Knolls Drive
Peoria, IL 61614-1083

ISBN 0-07-822610-4 [Lab Manual]

Printed in the United States of America

4 5 6 7 8 9 10 **024** 06 05 04 03

Contents

Chapter 6: Standards, Regulations & Laws

Chapter 7: Safety & Sanitation

Chapter 8: HACCP

Chapter 9: Equipment & Technology

Chapter 10: Knives & Smallwares

Chapter 11: Culinary Nutrition

Chapter 12: Creating Menus

Chapter 13: Using Standardized Recipes

Chapter 14: Cost Control

Chapter 15: Cooking Techniques

Chapter 16: Seasonings & Flavorings

Chapter 17: Breakfast Cookery

Chapter 18: Garde Manger

Chapter 19: Hot & Cold Sandwiches

Chapter 20: Stocks & Sauces

Chapter 21: Soups & Appetizers

Chapter 22: Fish & Shellfish

Chapter 23: Poultry Cookery

Chapter 24: Meat Cookery

Chapter 25: Pasta & Grains

Chapter 26: Ripening Fruit

Chapter 27: Baking Techniques

Chapter 28: Yeast Breads & Rolls

Chapter 29: Quick Breads

Chapter 30: Desserts

Credits

- Aero

- Cambro

- Detecto

- Friedr Dick Corporation

- Garland/A Welbilt Company

- Ann Garvin

- Gorman and Associates Inc.

- Hobart

- Steve Karp

- Matfer

- Ted Mishima

- Sitram

- Vote Photography

- Vulcan

Cover design: Squarecrow Creative Group
Interior design: Gorman & Associates Inc.

Foodservice Careers

Directions: Complete the table that follows by identifying available foodservice openings. An example has been provided to get you started. Describe the experience and training each job requires. For the wages, base your responses on average hourly wages in your community or on wage information you can find in the library or on the Internet.

Title	Job Responsibilities	Education/ Training	Wages
Line cook	Any duties necessary to prepare and produce menu items including cutting, portioning, cooking, and serving.	Vocational; on-the-job training	$8.00–$11.00/hour

Tracking Trends

Directions: Investigate trends for foodservice operations in your area. Choose at least three of the types of operations listed below. Identify at least three trends that impact each operation. Then, on a separate sheet of paper, describe how these trends compare to trends in similar foodservice operations in other areas of the country. Use the Internet and library resources for your research.

Quick-service restaurants	Full-service restaurants	Fine-dining restaurants
Hotels and resorts	Banquet facilities	Government facilities
On-site catering	Off-site catering	Bakeries and pastry shops

1. Type of operation:

A. _____

B. _____

C. _____

2. Type of operation:

A. _____

B. _____

C. _____

3. Type of operation:

A. _____

B. _____

C. _____

Developing a Career Plan

Directions: Complete the steps below to develop a career plan.

1. Using the Internet or your local newspaper's "Help Wanted" section, research the foodservice positions that are available in your community. List six jobs that appeal to you.

   _____   _____

   _____   _____

   _____   _____

2. Select one position to research, and attach a printed copy of the job description to this activity sheet.

3. Describe your current skills, work experience, and education that would help you obtain the job listed in step 2.

   _____

   _____

   _____

   _____

   _____

   _____

   _____

   _____

   _____

   _____

   _____

4. On a separate sheet of paper, write out a plan that shows the steps you would take to acquire the training, education, and experience needed to apply for this job. Be sure to include any entry-level jobs that would give you the basic skills or experience needed, and any work/study programs you might know about. Attach your plan to this activity sheet.

Business Plans

Directions: Work in teams to complete the steps below.

1. **Assign team roles.** Select one student to write down the major ideas in developing your business plan. Select another student to present your team's finished business plan to the class. The remaining team members should answer any questions after your presentation.

2. **Describe your foodservice business.** Your team may choose to start a fast-food restaurant, a family-style restaurant, or a catering company. Include the name of your foodservice business.

_____

_____

_____

_____

_____

_____

_____

_____

3. **State your vision.** Your team's vision statement should include:
   - Menu items
   - Start-up costs
   - Operating costs
   - Business location
   - Targeted customer base
   - Estimated profits

4. **Determine your goals.** Develop a list of major goals that need to be met. Your goals should be specific and measurable, and should include a timetable.

5. **Develop strategies.** Strategies are the roadmaps for meeting your goals. They provide direction. For example, strategies may include the type of marketing you will use to attract customers.

6. **Write your action plan.** Your action plan will help you reach your goals by providing a specific course of action.

7. **Present your business plan.** Answer any questions your classmates have about your presentation.

Writing a Letter of Request

Directions: Write a letter of request by completing the steps that follow.

1. Complete the chart below. In the first column, list everything you're good at.

2. In the second column, list the skills needed to become good at each item. For example, you may have listed that you are a good swimmer. The skills needed for this are commitment, discipline, and goal setting.

Things I'm Good At	Skills Needed To Do This Well
Swimming	Commitment, discipline, goal setting

(Continued on next page)

3. Look through the "Help Wanted" section of your local newspaper, and find a foodservice job listing that interests you. Attach it to this activity sheet.

4. Determine which skills in the job listing in step 2 would most benefit the employer in the job listing.

5. Write a letter of request to the employer. You may refer to the example in your textbook. Your letter of request should include a brief summary of your education, experience, and skills listed in step 2. Your letter of request should contain three paragraphs:
   - **First paragraph.** Introduce the purpose of the letter. For example, "I am looking for a position in a hotel where I can utilize my training in the culinary/hospitality arts. I would like a position with your hotel as a _____."
   - **Second paragraph.** Mention your qualifications for the job, including specific education (courses you have taken that relate to the position you are interested in), work experience, and leadership skills. Now add "voice" to your letter by taking one or two skills you listed in step 2, and include them in this letter. Write how these skills make you a more desirable employee candidate.
   - **Third paragraph.** Ask for an application form or an interview. State how you can be reached and when you will be available.

6. After you write your letter of request, read it out loud. Notice the voice and tone of the letter, and make any necessary changes.

7. Exchange your letter with a partner. Have your partner read your letter. Then make any final corrections.

8. Type the letter and attach it to this activity sheet for evaluation by your instructor.

Completing a Job Application

Directions: Fill out the job application below. Do not leave anything blank. If an entry is not applicable, write the letters NA.

Jonah's Eatery

Employment Application   Date: _____

PERSONAL DATA
Please print or type clearly.

Name _____
               Last Name   First Name   Middle Initial

Address _____ _____ _____ _____
               Street   City   State   Zip code

Telephone no. _____ **Social Security no.** _____

Are you legally entitled to work in the United States?   Yes ❑   No ❑

If hired, can you show proof of legal employment age?   Yes ❑   No ❑

Have you ever been convicted of a crime? If yes, please explain below.   Yes ❑   No ❑

_____

How were you referred to *Jonah's Eatery*?

School ❑   Advertisement ❑   Direct contact ❑   A Jonah's employee ❑

Other _____

Position Applying For _____

Applicable Skills _____

_____

_____

_____

(Continued on next page)

EDUCATIONAL DATA

School Type	School Name/Address	City/State
Senior High School		
College/University		
Graduate School		
Trade/Business/Night Courses		
Other		

EMPLOYMENT DATA   (List most recent jobs first.)

Employer _____ Employed from: ____ to: ____

Address _____ Wages or earnings _____

City _____ State ___ Zip code ___ (Area code) Telephone ____

Contact Name _____

Description of duties _____

_____

Reason for leaving or considering a change _____

_____

Employer _____ Employed from: ____ to: ____

Address _____ Wages or earnings _____

City _____ State ___ Zip code ___ (Area code) Telephone ____

Contact Name _____

Description of duties _____

_____

Reason for leaving or considering a change _____

_____

(Continued on next page)

Name _____ Date _____ LAB ACTIVITY 6
continued

Employer	Employed from: to:
Address	Wages or earnings
City State Zip code	(Area code) Telephone

Contact Name _____

Description of duties _____

_____

Reason for leaving or considering a change _____

_____

This employment application is not a contract and it is not meant to impose any legal obligation upon either you or Jonah's Eatery. If you are hired, your employment shall be "at will" and may be terminated at any time for any reason with or without prior notice or cause. Any oral statement or promises to the contrary are not binding upon the employer.

I confirm that all my answers to the questions in this employment application are accurate and complete. I also understand that the submission of any false information in connection with this employment application may be cause for immediate discharge at any time thereafter should I be employed by Jonah's Eatery. I understand that my employment will be contingent upon the accuracy, completeness, and acceptability of the information furnished to you. Permission is granted to Jonah's Eatery to verify all statements in this employment application. I understand my present employer will not be contacted until after I accept an offer of employment with Jonah's Eatery.

I have read the above statement and accept the same as a condition of my employment with Jonah's Eatery.

Signature: _____ **Date:** _____

Interviewing Skills

Directions: Read each statement in the chart below. Determine whether the behavior is appropriate and indicate this in the chart. If the behavior isn't appropriate, write in the correct behavior. An example has been completed for you.

Interview Behavior	Your Response
Lisa has an interview scheduled, but she didn't write down the information.	Inappropriate behavior. Always write down the date, time, and location of the interview, and ask for directions if necessary.
Michael wears jeans and a T-shirt to his interview.	
Nan arrives late for her interview, but it's because she got lost.	
Bill answered all the interview questions thoughtfully, but he didn't make eye contact.	
During her interview, Tamara slouches in her chair and fidgets with her hair.	
When asked a question, Min politely stated that she didn't know the answer.	
During the interview, Cody chews gum.	
Sarah was excited about her interview. She had many questions and asked them often, interrupting the interviewer.	
Dominic asked politely about the rate of pay and employee benefits.	
Barry thanked the interviewer for her time and asked when he could expect to hear back from her about the position.	
Marisa sent a thank-you note to the interviewer a week after the interview.	

Evaluating Job Offers

Directions: Read each situation below. Evaluate each job offer presented. Then decide which job offer should be accepted and explain why.

1. Marianne is a high school vocational-education student. She wants to be a chef someday. Marianne applied for several part-time jobs in foodservice to gain practical experience. She has received two job offers:

Job A	**Job B**
Fry station cook.	Hostess in a hotel dining room.

Which should she choose? Explain why.

_____

_____

2. Terrance is twenty-one and needs a full-time job to help pay for night school. He wants to work in foodservice, but isn't sure what he wants to do. He has received the following job offers:

Job A	**Job B**
Server working 40 hours per week at $4.75 an hour plus tips, which could increase his hourly rate to $12.00. He is required to be at work 40 hours whether or not the restaurant is busy.	Entry-level kitchen worker averaging 40 hours per week, making $360 per week. If business is slow, he doesn't have to come in, but still gets paid. Overtime may be required.

Which should he choose? Explain why.

_____

_____

_____

_____

_____

_____

_____

_____

(Continued on next page)

3. Ricardo is twenty-seven. He has held a variety of positions in foodservice, and prefers to work in the kitchen. He has received the following job offers:

Job A	**Job B**
An entry-level kitchen worker at a fish and sea-food restaurant averaging 40 hours per week.	Line cook at a coffeehouse that's only open from 4:00 am to noon.

Which should he choose? Explain why.

_____

_____

_____

_____

_____

4. Sabrina has eight years professional pastry chef experience. She is established in the community and is actively involved with local charities. She is seeking a position that offers her more responsibility, but she doesn't want to relocate. She has received the following job offers:

Job A	**Job B**
Assistant pastry chef at a local specialty establishment. Her responsibilities will increase, but so will the hours she works.	Head pastry chef at a hotel restaurant located 30 miles away. Her responsibility will increase, but her hours will not. She will, however, have to relocate or commute.

Which should she choose? Explain why.

_____

_____

_____

_____

_____

_____

Serving Customers

Directions: Working in teams, perform basic server skills as directed in the steps that follow.

1. **Greet customers.** Practice making eye contact and greeting customers. Use opening statements such as "Good afternoon. Welcome to the Culinary Connection." Ask one of the following questions: Do you have a reservation? How many will be in your party? Take turns being the host or server and customer.

2. **Present menus and take beverage orders.** Use the table and postion number drawings on page 73 of your textbook. Present the menus and take the beverage orders.

3. **Serve the beverage order.** Serve the beverages from the customer's right with your right hand.

4. **Take the food orders.** Use various sales techniques to take customer orders. Confirm each customer's order.

5. **Serve the customers following the order of service.** After taking the orders, serve bread. Then, serve the salads from the left side of the customer with your left hand.

6. **Clear the appropriate course.** Clear the table using your right hand from the customer's right side before serving the entrées.

7. **Serve the entrée orders.** Serve from the customer's left with your left hand.

8. **Check back with your customers.** Ask customers if they need anything.

9. **Clear the table.** Clear from the customer's right with your right hand.

10. **Thank your customers.** Use closing phrases, such as "How was your meal today?"

11. **Present the check.** Receive payment.

12. **Have your instructor complete the Performance Checklist on the next page.**

(Continued on next page)

Performance ✔ Checklist

Performance Standards
Level 4—Performs skill without supervision and adapts to problem situations.
Level 3—Performs skill satisfactorily without assistance or supervision.
Level 2—Performs skill satisfactorily, but requires assistance or supervision.
Level 1—Performs parts of skill satisfactorily, but requires considerable assistance or supervision.
Level 0—Cannot perform skill.

Attempt (circle one):   1   2   3   4

Comments: _____

_____

_____

_____

_____

Performance Level Achieved: _____

_____ 1. Host or server approaches customer promptly.

_____ 2. Host or server makes eye contact and greets customer cheerfully.

_____ 3. Host or server takes beverage order.

_____ 4. Host or server serves beverage from the right side using the right hand.

_____ 5. Server takes and confirms food order using sales techniques.

_____ 6. Server takes menus from customer.

_____ 7. Server serves bread followed by appetizers if ordered.

_____ 8. Server serves salad from the left side using the left hand.

_____ 9. Server clears appropriate courses using the right hand, from the right side before serving next course.

_____ 10. Server serves entrée from the left side using the left hand.

_____ 11. Server checks back periodically during and after meal to ask if the customer needs anything.

_____ 12. Server serves dessert from the left side using the correct utensil.

_____ 13. Server presents the check after clearing unnecessary items. Thanks customers and asks them to come back.

Instructor's Signature: _____   **Date:** _____

Service Skills

Directions: Perform the service skills that follow. Then have your instructor complete the Performance Checklist.

1. **Tray service.** Load a large service tray with dishes and glasses filled with water so it is balanced. Take turns properly lifting and carrying the tray to a table. Use a tray stand to place the tray on.

2. **Hand service.** Perform hand service by carrying three soup cups on your left arm and a fourth in your right hand and serve the soup. Then carry three plates on your right arm and a fourth in the left hand to your table and serve the entrées.

3. **Beverage service.** Perform beverage service for such beverages as coffee, hot tea, and iced tea. (*Note:* You can fill the beverage glassware, cups and saucers, or mugs with water.) Then practice serving the beverages using the correct procedure.

Performance ✔ Checklist

Performance Standards

Level 4—Performs skill without supervision and adapts to problem situations.

Level 3—Performs skill satisfactorily without assistance or supervision.

Level 2—Performs skill satisfactorily, but requires assistance or supervision.

Level 1—Performs parts of skill satisfactorily, but requires considerable assistance or supervision.

Level 0—Cannot perform skill.

Attempt (circle one):   1   2   3   4

Comments: _____

_____

_____

_____

_____

_____

Performance Level Achieved: _____

_____ 1. Properly loads a large service tray with dishes and glasses so it is balanced.

_____ 2. Uses a napkin for flatware, placing glasses right side up.

_____ 3. Lifts tray properly and balances it.

_____ 4. Demonstrates proper hand service by carrying four cups or plates.

_____ 5. Demonstrates beverage setup by preparing several types of beverages, such as coffee, hot tea, and iced tea.

_____ 6. Serves the beverages using the correct serviceware.

Instructor's Signature: _____   **Date:** _____

Setting a Cover

Directions: In the space provided below, draw and label the correct placement for the tableware for a dinner. Include all of the items listed below.

• Dinner plate	• Dinner knife	• Water glass
• Napkin	• Teaspoon	• Coffee cup and saucer
• Salad fork	• Bread-and-butter plate	• Dessert fork and spoon
• Dinner fork	• Butter knife	

Setting the Table

Directions: Follow the steps below for setting tables.

1. As a team, set two tables for six people. Place a centerpiece on each table to identify your team.

2. Use the Performance Checklist below to make sure your team's tables are set correctly.

3. Have your instructor complete the Performance Checklist.

Performance ✔ Checklist

Performance Standards

Level 4—Performs skill without supervision and adapts to problem situations.

Level 3—Performs skill satisfactorily without assistance or supervision.

Level 2—Performs skill satisfactorily, but requires assistance or supervision.

Level 1—Performs parts of skill satisfactorily, but requires considerable assistance or supervision.

Level 0—Cannot perform skill.

Attempt (circle one):   1   2   3   4

Comments: _____
_____
_____
_____
_____
_____

Performance Level Achieved: _____

_____ 1. Places chairs around table establishing each place setting.

_____ 2. Folds napkin and centers it on place setting.

_____ 3. Places flatware in the correct order of use and aligns it.

_____ 4. Correctly sets bread-and-butter plate.

_____ 5. Places water glass above the tip of the dinner knife.

_____ 6. Presets coffee and tea cups to the right of the knives and spoons. Positions handles correctly.

Instructor's Signature: _____   **Date:** _____

American Plated Service

Directions: Working in teams, perform American plated service by completing the steps that follow.

1. **Assign one member of your team to be the server.** The remaining team members will be the customers at the table. Take turns being the server until all team members have had an opportunity.
2. **Set a table for 4–6 people.**
3. **Present the menus.** Give each customer a menu and take the beverage orders.
4. **Serve the beverage orders.**
5. **Take the food orders.** Take each person's food order following the order of service for American plated service.
6. **Serve courses.** Serve each course to the customers using a tray and tray stand. The seated customers should not assist the server in presenting the plates.
7. **Clear between courses.** Clear the table between each course, preset appropriate flatware for the next course, and refresh the beverages as needed. Clear the table completely when your customers have finished eating.
8. **Thank your customers.**
9. **Present the check.**
10. **Have the instructor complete the Performance Checklist below at the end of service.**

Performance ✔ Checklist

Performance Standards
Level 4—Performs skill without supervision and adapts to problem situations.
Level 3—Performs skill satisfactorily without assistance or supervision.
Level 2—Performs skill satisfactorily, but requires assistance or supervision.
Level 1—Performs parts of skill satisfactorily, but requires considerable assistance or supervision.
Level 0—Cannot perform skill.

Attempt (circle one):   1   2   3   4

Comments: _____

_____

_____

_____

_____

_____

Performance Level Achieved: _____

_____ 1. Takes orders correctly following the order of service.

_____ 2. Executes American plated service according to the guidelines, demonstrating the use of a tray stand.

_____ 3. Refreshes beverages between courses.

_____ 4. Clears table properly, thanks customers, and presents check.

Instructor's Signature: _____ **Date:** _____

Culinary Essentials Lab Manual
Copyright © Glencoe/McGraw-Hill

Booth Service

Directions: Working in teams, perform booth service by completing the steps that follow.

1. **Assign one member of your team to be the server.** The remaining team members will be the customers at the table. Take turns being the server until all team members have had an opportunity.
2. **Set a table for 4–6 people.**
3. **Present the menus.** Give each customer a menu and take the beverage orders.
4. **Serve the beverage orders.**
5. **Take the food orders.** Take each person's food order following the order of service for booth service.
6. **Serve courses.** Serve each course to the customers using a tray and tray stand. The seated customers should not assist the server in presenting the plates.
7. **Clear between courses.** Clear the table between each course, preset appropriate flatware for the next course, and refresh the beverages as needed. Clear the table completely when your customers have finished eating.
8. **Thank your customers.**
9. **Present the check.**
10. **Have the instructor complete the Performance Checklist below at the end of service.**

Performance ✔ Checklist

Performance Standards
Level 4—Performs skill without supervision and adapts to problem situations.
Level 3—Performs skill satisfactorily without assistance or supervision.
Level 2—Performs skill satisfactorily, but requires assistance or supervision.
Level 1—Performs parts of skill satisfactorily, but requires considerable assistance or supervision.
Level 0—Cannot perform skill.

Attempt (circle one):   1   2   3   4

Comments: _____

_____

_____

_____

_____

_____

Performance Level Achieved: _____

_____ 1. Order was taken correctly following the order of service.

_____ 2. Booth service was executed according to the guidelines, demonstrating proper use of a focal point.

_____ 3. Service was provided without handing anything directly to the customers, but instead placing everything on the table in front of the appropriate customer.

_____ 4. Beverages were refreshed between courses using the right hand for serving.

_____ 5. Table was cleared, customers thanked, and the check properly presented.

Instructor's Signature: _____   **Date:** _____

Using a Serving Set

Directions: Practice handling a service set in one hand as is used in Russian service. Complete the steps that follow.

1. Review the diagram on the next page to observe the correct placement of the service set for Russian service.

2. Place the tablespoon on the last three fingers of the hand that you will be using. The little finger goes on top of the spoon handle, as shown in the diagram.

3. Pick up the fork using your forefinger and thumb.

4. Practice moving the fork and tablespoon until they come together at the end of the spoon and fork tines. You should be able to click the ends together.

5. Practice picking up and moving a variety of items from one place to another, including items that are flat, round, light, heavy, and awkward.

6. Place a food item in a sauté pan only using Russian service to move, turn, and dish the product.

7. Demonstrate your skill for your instructor.

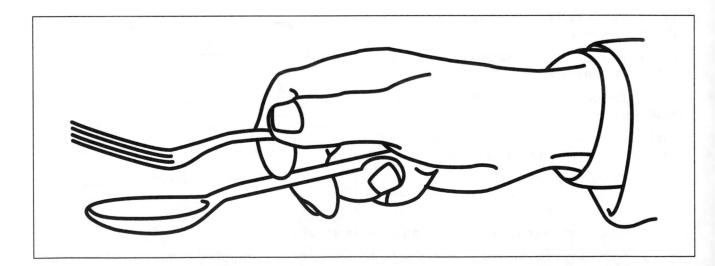

Using Russian Service

Directions: In teams, practice Russian service according to the following steps:

1. Practice Russian service. Assign one team member to be the server. The other team members will be the guests at the table. Each student will take a turn being the server.
2. The server should bring the entrée and the rest of the meal.
3. Serve each item from the service plates or platters held in the left hand to the customers using serving sets in the right hand.
4. Clear the table.
5. Have the instructor complete the Performance Checklist below.

Performance ✔ Checklist

Performance Standards

Level 4—Performs skill without supervision and adapts to problem situations.

Level 3—Performs skill satisfactorily without assistance or supervision.

Level 2—Performs skill satisfactorily, but requires assistance or supervision.

Level 1—Performs parts of skill satisfactorily, but requires considerable assistance or supervision.

Level 0—Cannot perform skill.

Attempt (circle one):   1   2   3   4

Comments: _____

_____

_____

_____

_____

_____

Performance Level Achieved: _____

_____ 1. Russian service concept was understood.

_____ 2. The fork and tablespoon were held correctly.

_____ 3. Russian service was performed correctly.

_____ 4. Serving plates and platters were presented correctly.

_____ 5. Russian service was executed according to the guidelines, and service moved counterclockwise.

_____ 6. Server had a clean napkin draped over the left forearm.

_____ 7. Empty plates and bowls were placed in front of the customer from the right side.

_____ 8. Items were served to the customer with the right hand from the customer's left side.

_____ 9. The server stood with his or her left foot forward while serving the customer.

_____ 10. The serving set was used correctly.

_____ 11. Items were removed from the table with the server's right hand from the customer's right side.

Instructor's Signature: _____   **Date:** _____

Name _____ Date _____

Folding the Bishop's Hat

Directions: Practice folding the Bishop's Hat following the diagrams below. When you have perfected folding the Bishop's Hat, perform this skill for your instructor. Have your instructor complete the Performance Checklist below.

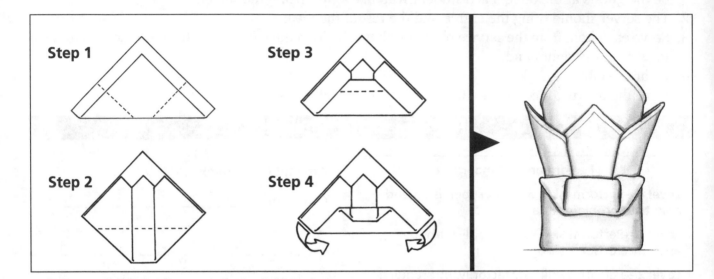

Step 1

Step 2

Step 3

Step 4

Performance ✔ Checklist

Performance Standards

Level 4—Performs skill without supervision and adapts to problem situations.

Level 3—Performs skill satisfactorily without assistance or supervision.

Level 2—Performs skill satisfactorily, but requires assistance or supervision.

Level 1—Performs parts of skill satisfactorily, but requires considerable assistance or supervision.

Level 0—Cannot perform skill.

Attempt (circle one):   1   2   3   4

Comments: _____

_____

_____

_____

_____

_____

Performance Level Achieved: _____

_____ 1. Napkin folds are accurate and crisp.

_____ 2. Napkin folds follow the illustrated steps and interlock properly.

_____ 3. Bishop's Hat napkin stands properly on the table.

Instructor's Signature: _____ **Date:** _____

Folding the Flaming Flower

Directions: Practice folding the Flaming Flower following the diagrams below. When you have perfected folding the Flaming Flower, perform this skill for your instructor. Have your instructor complete the Performance Checklist below.

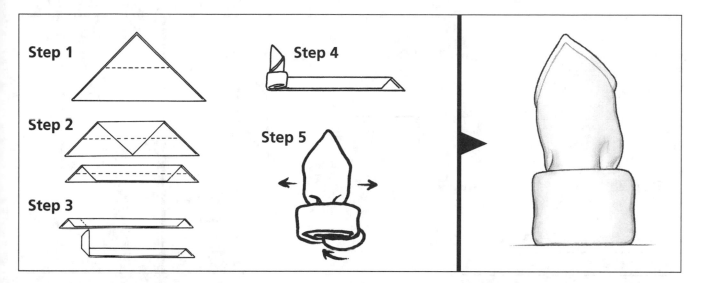

Step 1
Step 2
Step 3
Step 4
Step 5

Performance ✔ Checklist

Performance Standards

Level 4—Performs skill without supervision and adapts to problem situations.

Level 3—Performs skill satisfactorily without assistance or supervision.

Level 2—Performs skill satisfactorily, but requires assistance or supervision.

Level 1—Performs parts of skill satisfactorily, but requires considerable assistance or supervision.

Level 0—Cannot perform skill.

Attempt (circle one):   1   2   3   4

Comments: _____

_____

_____

_____

_____

Performance Level Achieved: _____

_____ 1. Napkin folds are accurate and crisp.

_____ 2. Napkin folds follow the illustrated steps and interlock properly.

_____ 3. Flaming Flower napkin stands properly on the table.

Instructor's Signature: _____   **Date:** _____

Folding the Candlestick

Directions: Practice folding the Candlestick following the diagrams below. When you have perfected folding the Candlestick, perform this skill for your instructor. Have your instructor complete the Performance Checklist below.

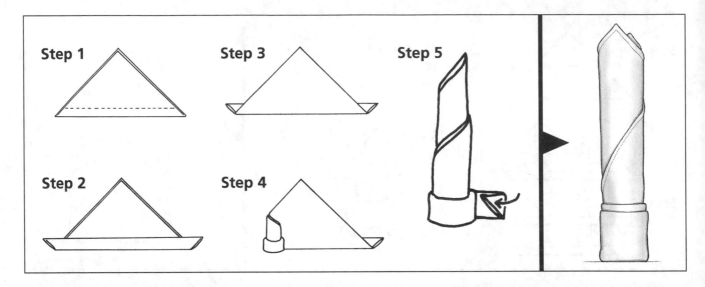

Step 1   Step 3   Step 5

Step 2   Step 4

Performance ✔ Checklist

Performance Standards

Level 4—Performs skill without supervision and adapts to problem situations.

Level 3—Performs skill satisfactorily without assistance or supervision.

Level 2—Performs skill satisfactorily, but requires assistance or supervision.

Level 1—Performs parts of skill satisfactorily, but requires considerable assistance or supervision.

Level 0—Cannot perform skill.

Attempt (circle one):   1   2   3   4

Comments: _____
_____
_____
_____
_____
_____

Performance Level Achieved: _____

_____ 1. Napkin folds are accurate and crisp.

_____ 2. Napkin folds follow the illustrated steps and interlock properly.

_____ 3. Candlestick napkin stands properly on the table.

Instructor's Signature: _____   **Date:** _____

Folding Twin Peaks

Directions: Practice folding the Twin Peaks following the diagrams below. When you have perfected folding the Twin Peaks, perform this skill for your instructor. Have your instructor complete the Performance Checklist below.

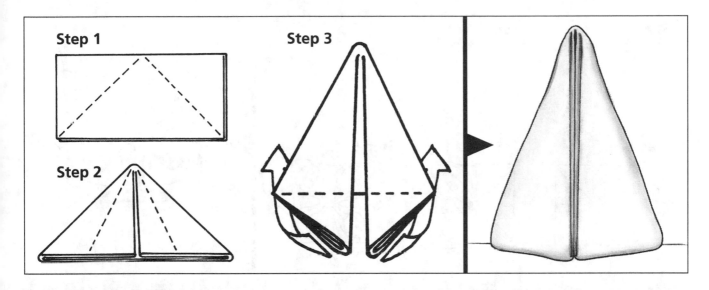

Performance ✔ Checklist

Performance Standards	
Level 4—Performs skill without supervision and adapts to problem situations.	
Level 3—Performs skill satisfactorily without assistance or supervision.	
Level 2—Performs skill satisfactorily, but requires assistance or supervision.	
Level 1—Performs parts of skill satisfactorily, but requires considerable assistance or supervision.	
Level 0—Cannot perform skill.	

Attempt (circle one):   1   2   3   4

Comments: _____

_____

_____

_____

_____

_____

Performance Level Achieved: _____

_____ 1. Napkin folds are accurate and crisp.

_____ 2. Napkin folds follow the illustrated steps and interlock properly.

_____ 3. Twin Peaks napkin stands properly on the table.

Instructor's Signature: _____   **Date:** _____

Folding the Water Lily

Directions: Practice folding the Water Lily following the diagrams below. When you have perfected folding the Water Lily, perform this skill for your instructor. Have your instructor complete the Performance Checklist below.

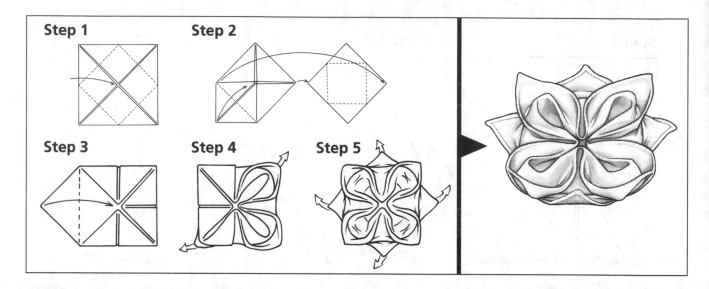

Step 1   Step 2   Step 3   Step 4   Step 5

Performance ✔ Checklist

Performance Standards
Level 4—Performs skill without supervision and adapts to problem situations.
Level 3—Performs skill satisfactorily without assistance or supervision.
Level 2—Performs skill satisfactorily, but requires assistance or supervision.
Level 1—Performs parts of skill satisfactorily, but requires considerable assistance or supervision.
Level 0—Cannot perform skill.

Attempt (circle one):   1   2   3   4

Comments: _____

_____

_____

_____

_____

_____

Performance Level Achieved: _____

_____ 1. Napkin folds are accurate and crisp.

_____ 2. Napkin folds follow the illustrated steps, with the petals and leaves properly formed.

_____ 3. Water Lily lays properly on the table, with petals turned slightly upward and napkin corners forming the leaves between the petals.

Instructor's Signature: _____   **Date:** _____

Managing Foodservice Staff

Directions: Determine the appropriate management response for each situation that follows. Use a separate sheet of paper if necessary and attach it to this sheet.

1. **Reassessing staffing needs.** A line cook calls in sick. What should you do?

_____

_____

_____

2. **Covering the shift.** It's the noon rush, and you're short staffed. You can't call anyone else in. How do you cover the shift?

_____

_____

_____

3. **Handling customer complaints.** Working in teams, role-play a situation in which a customer has a complaint about the service or quality of food in a restaurant. Take turns being the customer, server, and manager. The server's role is to determine what the customer's complaint is and explain it to the manager. The manager should then attempt to resolve the problem, demonstrating both tact and fairness. Evaluate each other's responses as manager.

4. **Controling cost.** Flatware is disappearing at the end of the day. How can you address this issue?

_____

_____

_____

5. **Replacing staff.** Three employees have given you two weeks' notice. One other employee no longer shows up for work. What should you do?

_____

_____

_____

_____

Production Schedules

Directions: The chart below shows a typical production schedule for meal preparation and service. Complete the chart by filling in preparation start times for each menu item.

Lunch Production Schedule—11:00 a.m. to 2:00 p.m.			
Item	**Portions**	**Work Station**	**Start Time**
Country Fried Steak with Gravy	25	Fry Station	
New Potatoes	25	Hot Station	
Green Beans	25	Hot Station	
Cloverleaf Rolls	50	Bake Station	
Strawberry Shortcake	25	Bake Station	
Mixed Greens with Ranch Dressing	25	Garde Manger Station	
Coffee and Iced Tea	50	Beverage Station and Servers	
Kitchen Clean-up		Dishwashing Station	
Floater		Floater	

Culinary Essentials Lab Manual
Copyright © Glencoe/McGraw-Hill

Sanitation & Safety Inspections

Directions: Select five chemicals used in your commercial kitchen laboratory. Read the material safety data sheets for these chemicals. Then complete the chart that follows.

Chemical Name	Equipment Used On	Safety Precautions

Name _____ Date _____

The Americans with Disabilities Act

Directions: Review The Americans with Disabilities Act. Then complete the steps that follow.

Part A

1. Evaluate your restaurant dining room to see if it meets The Americans with Disabilities Act requirements. Look for other obstacles that a person with a disability might have to overcome to move around the dining room. What can you change or alter to make entry and seating more accessible for people with disabilities? List your suggestions on a separate sheet of paper and attach it to this activity sheet.

Part B

1. Work with a partner and take turns being a disabled employee and observer. Select one of the following disabilities:

   • No left hand or forearm   • Walks with a cane

   • Blind   • Deaf

2. Choose one of the following scenarios:

   • A disabled foodservice handler needs to prepare side garden salads for lunch.

   • A disabled bread baker needs to measure, mix, and bake a quick bread.

   • A disabled dishwasher needs to scrape, rinse, rack, and wash dishes in the dishwasher.

   • A disabled assistant cook needs to plate food on the hot line.

   • A disabled grill person needs to grill 3 hamburgers served with French fries and plated with condiments.

   One person will be the disabled employee and role-play the task described in the selected scenario. The other person will be the observer and record the difficulties faced by the disabled employee. On a separate sheet of paper, the observer should record the following information:

   • Employee name, observer name, type of disability, and which scenario above is used.

   • List the tasks that were easy for the disabled person to accomplish.

   • List the tasks that were moderately hard for the disabled person to accomplish.

   • List the tasks that were hard or impossible for the disabled person to accomplish.

   • Suggest adjustments that could be made to make each task easier to perform based on the disability.

   • What conclusions can you draw from this activity?

3. Share both sets of observations with the class. Discuss what conclusions you can draw from this activity. Can adaptations be made in your commercial kitchen laboratory to accommodate someone with a disability? Do some stations work better than others?

Fire Safety

Directions, Part A: The drawing below shows a typical medium-sized restaurant. Draw a quick and safe path showing how to exit the restaurant in the event of a fire. In creating your fire exit plan, be sure to:

• Use a colored pen or pencil to draw the paths people should take to the fire exits.

• Indicate where all fire exits are located.

• Mark the locations of all fire extinguishers.

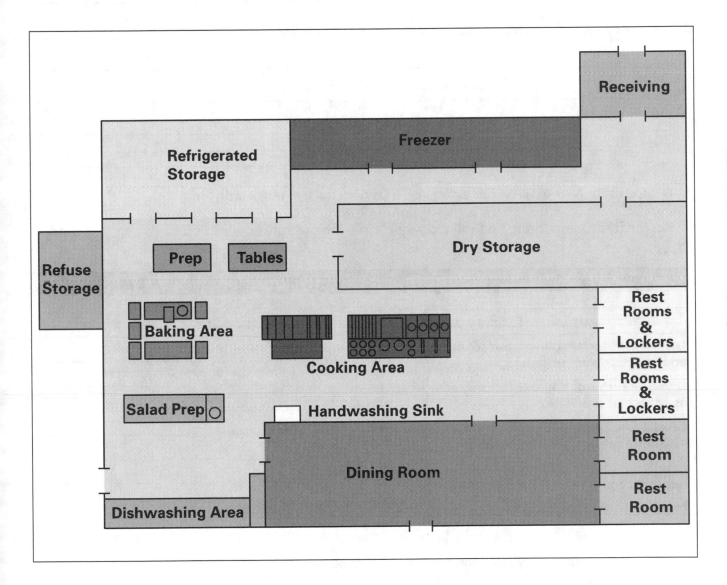

(Continued on next page)

Directions, Part B: Respond to the following statements and demonstrate the following procedures as directed by your instructor.

1. Describe the procedure for responding to a fire.

_____

_____

_____

2. List the classes of fires and which fire extinguisher to use for each.

_____

_____

_____

_____

3. Demonstrate how to use a fire extinguisher as directed by your instructor.

4. Research the "stop, drop, and roll technique" and demonstrate how it is used.

Performance ✔ Checklist

Performance Standards

Level 4—Performs skill without supervision and adapts to problem situations.

Level 3—Performs skill satisfactorily without assistance or supervision.

Level 2—Performs skill satisfactorily, but requires assistance or supervision.

Level 1—Performs parts of skill satisfactorily, but requires considerable assistance or supervision.

Level 0—Cannot perform skill.

Attempt (circle one): 1 2 3 4

Comments: _____

_____

_____

_____

_____

Performance Level Achieved: _____

_____ 1. Follows fire safety rules and practices at all times.

_____ 2. Demonstrates proper use of a fire extinguisher.

_____ 3. Demonstrates the correct procedure for the stop, drop, and roll technique.

Instructor's Signature: _____ **Date:** _____

Contamination Hazards

Directions: Read the description in each item that follows. Then, fill out the chart by identifying:
• The type of contamination—direct contamination or cross-contamination.
• The cause of contamination.
• How the contamination could have been prevented.

Receiving Area

Item 1: Cartons of corn on a delivery truck are discolored and unshucked cobs are covered with a film.
Item 2: A carton of chicken breasts has been left out on a work table for 7 hours.

Type of Contamination	Cause of Contamination	Preventive Measures
Item 1		
Item 2		

Preparation Area

Item 3: A 10-lb. block of cheese in the refrigerator is growing green, fuzzy spots.
Item 4: A cook sneezes on the hamburgers he is preparing.

Type of Contamination	Cause of Contamination	Preventive Measures
Item 3		
Item 4		

Types of Contamination

Directions: Complete the chart below by following steps 1 and 2.

1. List the sources of and foods associated with each type of contamination.

2. Describe the precautions and sanitation procedures that can lower the risk of contamination.

Contamination	Foods Often Affected	Precautions	Sanitation Procedures
Bacteria			
Viruses			
Parasites			
Molds			

Potential Hazards

Directions: List the main areas of your lab. Then identify the potential biological, chemical, and physical hazards in each area. Use the chart below to list potential hazards and prevention methods for each area. An example has been given.

Lab Area	Type of Hazard	Prevention Method
Sinks	Mold—Biological hazard	Clean sink area; wash and sanitize dishes.

Hand-Washing Experiment

Directions: Investigate the role of proper hand-washing in eliminating cross-contamination by completing the steps that follow.

1. Prior to washing your hands, collect scrapings from under your fingernails.

2. Place these fingernail scrapings into the growing medium in a petri dish to observe. Label this dish "Sample A," then store it in a safe place as directed by your instructor.

3. Review the steps on page 180 of your textbook on proper hand-washing. Then wash your hands following this procedure.

4. After washing your hands, collect additional scrapings from under your fingernails.

5. Put these fingernail scrapings into the growing medium in a second petri dish to observe. Label this dish "Sample B," then store it in a safe place as directed by your instructor.

6. Check the fingernail scrapings in each of the petri dishes after 24 hours. Then check the petri dishes again after 48, and again after 72 hours.

7. Record the changes found in each petri dish. How do the fingernail scrapings compare? What impact did hand-washing have on Sample B?

8. Practice the hand-washing procedure several more times after you have completed the fingernail scraping experiment. Then complete the Performance Checklist below.

Performance ✔ Checklist

Performance Standards
Level 4—Performs skill without supervision and adapts to problem situations.
Level 3—Performs skill satisfactorily without assistance or supervision.
Level 2—Performs skill satisfactorily, but requires assistance or supervision.
Level 1—Performs parts of skill satisfactorily, but requires considerable assistance or supervision.
Level 0—Cannot perform skill.

Attempt (circle one):   1   2   3   4

Comments: _____

_____

_____

_____

_____

_____

Performance Level Achieved: _____

_____ 1. Safety and sanitation practices were followed at all times during this job.

_____ 2. This completed job met the standards and was done within the allotted time.

Instructor's Signature: _____ **Date:** _____

Name _____ Date _____

HACCP

Directions: Create a poster on sanitation know-how by completing the following steps:

1. Choose a topic from the chart below.

2. Research information about your topic from the textbook and other print or Internet resources available to you.

3. Check out the area in your commercial kitchen laboratory that covers your topic. Inspect the area, noting any potential hazards for foods. Then identify safe methods for handling food in the area.

4. Prepare the information and visuals for the "Are You Sanitation Smart?" poster for your area.

5. Share the poster with the class. Have your instructor complete the Performance Checklist.

Topic	Checklist
Hand-washing	✔ Check sink. ✔ Soap available. ✔ Sanitizer available. ✔ Use proper hand-washing techniques.
Potentially hazardous foods	✔ Milk & milk products. ✔ Shell eggs. ✔ Poultry. ✔ Beef, pork, lamb. ✔ Fish, shellfish. ✔ Soy-protein foods, tofu. ✔ Melons (sliced). ✔ Garlic & oil mixtures. ✔ Cooked rice.
Storeroom	✔ Inspect. ✔ Follow FIFO rotation. ✔ Check labeling and dating.
Refrigerator	✔ Store cooked and raw foods properly. ✔ Check rotation, labeling, and dating.
Freezer	✔ Check labeling and dating. ✔ Wrap food; shelf life.

(Continued on next page)

Topic	Checklist
Cook's station	✔ Thaw foods in the refrigerator. ✔ Achieve minimal internal temperatures of cooked products. ✔ Achieve proper reheating temperature. ✔ Monitor steam table holding time. ✔ Avoid temperature danger zone. ✔ Cool foods properly.
Manual Dishwashing	✔ Scrape. ✔ Pre-rinse. ✔ Wash. ✔ Rinse. ✔ Sanitize. ✔ Use test strips. ✔ Air dry.
Dishwasher	✔ Scrape. ✔ Soak. ✔ Rinse. ✔ Wash. ✔ Rinse. ✔ Sanitize. ✔ Use drying agent.

Performance ✔ Checklist

Performance Standards

Level 4—Performs skill without supervision and adapts to problem situations.

Level 3—Performs skill satisfactorily without assistance or supervision.

Level 2—Performs skill satisfactorily, but requires assistance or supervision.

Level 1—Performs parts of skill satisfactorily, but requires considerable assistance or supervision.

Level 0—Cannot perform skill.

Attempt (circle one): 1 2 3 4

Comments: _____

_____

_____

_____

_____

Performance Level Achieved: _____

_____ 1. Sanitation posters follow HACCP guidelines.

Instructor's Signature: _____ **Date:** _____

Time & Temperature Safety

Directions: Complete each of the following activities to ensure food safety.

Calibrating a Thermometer

1. Insert the bottom half of an instant-read thermometer stem into a small container of equal parts of ice and cold water. Allow the thermometer to rest.

2. Read the temperature. The thermometer should read 32°F.

3. Adjust the calibration nut until the thermometer reads 32°F if the temperature reading in Step 2 is not 32°F.

Researching Safe Cooked-Food Temperatures

1. Research safe cooked-food temperatures using your textbook and government resources.

2. Complete the Minimum Safe Internal Cooking & Holding Time & Temperature Chart on page 48.

Testing Cooked & Held Food

1. Using the Minimum Safe Internal Cooking & Holding Time & Temperature Chart on page 48 as a guide, prepare a creamed and a clear soup.

2. Test the soups for the minimum safe internal temperature for serving. Use the Time and Temperature Checklist on page 49 to record results.

3. Hold the soups in a steam table or bain marie. Test the holding temperature after 1 hour and then again after 2 hours. Record the temperatures on the Hot & Cold Holding & Cooking Temperature Chart. Did the soup become overcooked due to long holding time and/or high amount of heat on the steam table? If soups do not meet the minimum holding temperatures, suggest remedies to maintain food safety. Write your responses on a separate sheet of paper.

4. Cool the soups for storage using the two-stage cooling method. Use the Hot and Cold Holding & Cooking Temperature Chart on page 49 to record the temperatures of soups as they are being cooled for storage. Record the temperature every fifteen minutes to test how the internal temperature decreases as the soup cools. What adjustments need to be made in cooling and holding equipment to maintain a safe temperature?

Washing & Sanitizing Cooking Equipment

1. Fill a three-compartment pot and pan sink. The left sink is for washing, the middle sink is for rinsing, and the right sink is for sanitizing.

2. Test the temperature of the water in the sanitizing sink.

(Continued on next page)

3. Record the information according to the type of sanitizing solution used in your commercial kitchen laboratory. Use the test strips to record the ppm, or parts per million. Make any adjustments to meet industry standards, and report the results to the class.

Type of sanitizer: _____   Registered ppm: _____

Did you need to make any adjustments to meet industry standards? If so, describe those adjustments on a separate sheet of paper.

4. Clean all the equipment used to prepare the soups and store appropriately.

Safe Internal Cooking & Holding Time & Temperature Chart	
Food Item	**Minimum Safe Internal Temperature & Time**
Fish	_____ °F for 15 seconds.
Beef roasts	_____ °F for 15 seconds; 140°F if maintained for 12 minutes; or 130°F if maintained for 121 minutes.
Cooked eggs	_____ °F for at least 15 seconds. If eggs cannot be cooked, use pasteurized eggs in recipe.
Pork & injected meats	_____ °F for 15 seconds.
Game meats— commercially dressed game	_____ °F for at least 15 seconds.
Chopped, ground, flaked, or minced meats.	_____ °F for at least 15 seconds.
Pork, sausage & injected meats, bacon	_____ °F for 15 seconds.
Poultry, stuffed meats, and stuffed pastas	_____ °F for 15 seconds. Cook stuffing separately.
Reheating of foods	_____ °F for 15 seconds within 2 hours.
Stuffing	_____ °F for at least 15 seconds.
Microwave cooking of meat, poultry, fish	_____ °F or above. Let stand 2 minutes to equalize the temperature. Take the temperature in two areas to determine internal temperature.

(Continued on next page)

Time & Temperature Checklist

Food Item	Safe Temperature Reading	Actual Temperature Reading	Remedy

Hot & Cold Holding & Cooling Temperature Chart

Food Item	1st Time	2nd Time	3rd Time	4th Time	5th Time

Performance ✔ Checklist

Performance Standards

Level 4—Performs skill without supervision and adapts to problem situations.

Level 3—Performs skill satisfactorily without assistance or supervision.

Level 2—Performs skill satisfactorily, but requires assistance or supervision.

Level 1—Performs parts of skill satisfactorily, but requires considerable assistance or supervision.

Level 0—Cannot perform skill.

Attempt (circle one):   1   2   3   4

Comments: _____
_____
_____
_____
_____
_____

Performance Level Achieved: _____

_____ 1. Proper procedure was followed for calibrating an instant-read thermometer.

_____ 2. Safety and sanitation practices were followed at all times during this job.

_____ 3. Temperature readings were taken accurately through all parts of the activity.

_____ 4. Equipment was cleaned and sanitized properly.

_____ 5. This completed job met the standards and was done within the allotted time.

Instructor's Signature: _____ **Date:** _____

Kitchen Workflow

Directions: Walk through the lab kitchen. If your lab is not set up like a commercial facility, tour the school cafeteria kitchen. Make suggestions for change that might better organize the kitchen facility, such as overhead and undercounter storage units (type, material, and size) and any related safety and lighting requirements. Record your suggestions below.

_____

_____

_____

_____

_____

_____

_____

_____

_____

_____

_____

_____

_____

_____

_____

_____

_____

_____

_____

_____

_____

Identifying Commercial Equipment

Directions: Label the following pieces of commercial foodservice equipment. To the right of each photo, list at least three ways in which you could use each piece of equipment. Follow the example as shown below.

Example:

- Purée soups
- Shred vegetables
- Crush garlic

Food Processor

- _____
- _____
- _____
- _____

1. _____

- _____
- _____
- _____
- _____

2. _____

- _____
- _____
- _____
- _____

3. _____

- _____
- _____
- _____
- _____

4. _____

(Continued on next page)

- _____
- _____
- _____
- _____

- _____
- _____
- _____
- _____

5. _____

6. _____

- _____
- _____
- _____
- _____

- _____
- _____
- _____
- _____

7. _____

8. _____

- _____
- _____
- _____
- _____

- _____
- _____
- _____
- _____

9. _____

10. _____

(Continued on next page)

- _____
- _____
- _____
- _____

- _____
- _____
- _____
- _____

11. _____

12. _____

- _____
- _____
- _____
- _____

- _____
- _____
- _____
- _____

13. _____

14. _____

- _____
- _____
- _____
- _____

- _____
- _____
- _____
- _____

15. _____

16. _____

Knife Construction

Directions: Label the parts of the knife as shown in the drawing below.

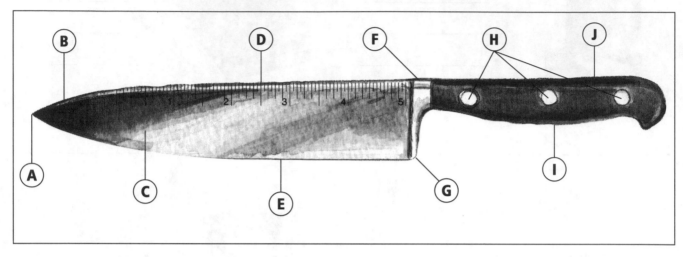

A. _____

B. _____

C. _____

D. _____

E. _____

F. _____

G. _____

H. _____

I. _____

J. _____

Name _____ Date _____

Type of Knives

Directions: Identify each knife shown by writing its name in the space beneath each photo. To the right of each photo, describe the tasks for which the knife should be used.

1. _____

2. _____

3. _____

4. _____

5. _____

6. _____

7. _____

8. _____

Culinary Essentials Lab Manual
Copyright © Glencoe/McGraw-Hill

55

Name _____ Date _____

Knife Cuts

Directions: Use the following steps to complete this activity:

1. In the chart that follows, write the name of the correct knife to use when making each of the cuts listed.

2. Using carrots or potatoes, practice making each of the cuts listed. Refer to pages 236-237 and page 587 in your text as a guide.

3. Check the size of your final cuts to be sure they match the measurements listed in the chart.

4. Once you are comfortable making each of the cuts correctly, demonstrate the cuts as selected and directed by your instructor.

A. French fry _____

B. Stick _____

C. Baton _____

D. Julienne _____

E. Fine matchstick _____

F. Large dice _____

G. Medium dice _____

H. Small dice _____

I. Round _____

J. Diagonal _____

Culinary Essentials Lab Manual
Copyright © Glencoe/McGraw-Hill

Name _____ Date _____

Identifying Smallwares

Directions: Use the following steps to identify a variety of smallwares and their uses:

1. In the space provided, identify each smallware by its proper name.
2. Indicate how and for which tasks each smallware would be used.

1. _____

2. _____

3. _____

4. _____

5. _____

6. _____

(Continued on next page)

Culinary Essentials Lab Manual
Copyright © Glencoe/McGraw-Hill

7. _____

8. _____

9. _____

10. _____

11. _____

12. _____

13. _____

14. _____

(Continued on next page)

Name _____ Date _____

_____
_____
_____
_____

15. _____

_____
_____
_____
_____

16. _____

_____
_____
_____
_____

17. _____

_____
_____
_____
_____

18. _____

_____
_____
_____
_____

19. _____

_____
_____
_____
_____

20. _____

_____
_____
_____
_____

21. _____

_____
_____
_____
_____

22. _____

(Continued on next page)

23. _____

24. _____

25. _____

26. _____

27. _____

28. _____

29. _____

30. _____

Food Labels

Directions: Review the two product nutrition labels below and answer the questions that follow.

Reduced-Fat Product		
Name of product: reduced-fat milk		
Serving size: 1 cup		
Servings per container: 1		
Calories per serving: 120		
Calories from fat per serving: 45		
Total fat:	5g	8% DV
Saturated fat:	3g	15% DV
Cholesterol:	20mg	7% DV
Sodium:	120mg	5% DV
Total carbohydrate:	11g	4% DV
Dietary fiber:	0g	0% DV
Sugars:	11g	
Protein:	9g	17% DV
Vitamin A:		10% DV
Vitamin C:		4% DV
Calcium:		30% DV
Iron:		25% DV

Nonfat Product		
Name of product: nonfat milk		
Serving size: 1 cup		
Servings per container: 1		
Calories per serving: 80		
Calories from fat per serving: 0		
Total fat:	0g	0% DV
Saturated fat:	0g	0% DV
Cholesterol:	less than 5mg	0% DV
Sodium:	120mg	5% DV
Total carbohydrate:	11g	4% DV
Dietary fiber:	0g	0% DV
Sugars:	11g	
Protein:	9g	17% DV
Vitamin A:		10% DV
Vitamin C:		4% DV
Calcium:		30% DV
Iron:		25% DV

1. What differences do you notice in the nutritional values for these two products?

   _____

   _____

2. Why is it important to be able to read and understand food labels in a foodservice operation?

   _____

   _____

   _____

(Continued on next page)

3. Based on the nutrition information listed on the food labels on page 61, which product is a more healthful option? Explain why.

_____

_____

_____

_____

_____

_____

4. Identify ways each food product might be used in a foodservice operation.

_____

_____

_____

_____

_____

_____

_____

5. How might the number of servings in each product impact the portion size of a menu item?

_____

_____

_____

_____

_____

_____

_____

_____

(Continued on next page)

6. Select a reduced-fat and nonfat food item and compare nutritional information by completing the food labels below.

Reduced-Fat Food		
Name of product: _____		
Serving size: _____		
Servings per container: _____		
Calories per serving: _____		
Calories from fat per serving: _____		
Total fat:	g	% DV
Saturated fat:	g	% DV
Cholesterol:	mg	% DV
Sodium:	mg	% DV
Total carbohydrate:	g	% DV
Dietary fiber:	g	% DV
Sugars:	g	
Protein:	g	% DV
Vitamin A:		% DV
Vitamin C:		% DV
Calcium:		% DV
Iron:		% DV

Nonfat Food		
Name of product: _____		
Serving size: _____		
Servings per container: _____		
Calories per serving: _____		
Calories from fat per serving: _____		
Total fat:	g	% DV
Saturated fat:	g	% DV
Cholesterol:	mg	% DV
Sodium:	mg	% DV
Total carbohydrate:	g	% DV
Dietary fiber:	g	% DV
Sugars:	g	
Protein:	g	% DV
Vitamin A:		% DV
Vitamin C:		% DV
Calcium:		% DV
Iron:		% DV

7. Based on the information in your food labels, which food item is the healthier choice? Explain why.

_____

_____

_____

_____

8. How might this food item be used in foodservice?

_____

_____

_____

_____

Many Nutritious Menu Options

Directions: On the line following each of the nutrients below, write the effect that nutrient is likely to have on the body. Then, on the "Chef's choice" line, list two food sources containing this nutrient that are good menu options.

1. Proteins: _____

    Chef's choice complete proteins: _____

    _____

    Chef's choice incomplete protein combinations that form complete proteins: _____

    _____

2. Carbohydrates: _____

    Chef's choice of complex carbohydrates: _____

    _____

    Chef's choice of simple carbohydrates: _____

3. Fats: _____

    Chef's choice of monounsaturated fats: _____

    Chef's choice of polyunsaturated fats: _____

    _____

4. Vitamins A, D, E, and K: _____

    _____

    Chef's choice for Vitamins A, D, E, and K: _____

    _____

    _____

5. Vitamins B and C: _____

    _____

    _____

    Chef's choice for Vitamins B and C: _____

    _____

    _____

Evaluating Food Choices

Directions: Use the United States Department of Agriculture (USDA), Center for Nutrition Policy and Promotion Web site or another diet analysis program to complete the steps that follow.

1. Review the menus that follow.

MENU A—JUST FOR KIDS

Soups

Tomato Soup . . . . Cup $1.75   Vegetable Pasta Soup . . . . Cup $1.75
Bowl $3.25   Bowl $3.25

Salads

House Salad. $2.95
Baby mixed greens, Roma tomatoes, julienne carrots,
and cucumbers served with ranch dressing.

Cole slaw $1.25
A mixture of shredded green and red cabbage, carrots, and dressing.

Entrées

Hot Dog and Fries. $1.95
Grilled hot dog and bun served with a side of crinkle-cut French fries.

Chicken Planks and Fries $3.65
Deep fried boneless chicken breast served with sweet
and sour sauce and crinkle-cut French fries.

Ravioli $3.25
A blend of three cheeses—Ricotta, mozzarella, and provolone
—stuffed in ravioli and covered with tomato sauce.
Served with a slice of garlic bread.

Grilled Cheese Sandwich and Fries $2.95
American cheese melted between thick slices of sourdough bread
and served with crinkle-cut French fries.

(Continued on next page)

MENU B—THE GARDEN SPOT

Appetizers & Soups

Black Bean Nachos $4.25	Vegetable Pasta Soup . . . . Cup $1.75
Potato Skins. $3.75	Bowl $3.25
Steamed Vegetable Medley $3.75	Tomato Soup . . . . Cup $1.75
Pasta Salad $4.25	Bowl $3.25

Salads

Blackened Tofu Salad $7.95
  An enticing mixture of tofu, shiitake mushrooms, and couscous.

The Garden Spot House Salad $4.95
  Baby mixed greens, Roma tomatoes, and feta cheese
  with balsamic vinaigrette.

Entrées

Vegetable Terrine $9.95
  Carrots, collard greens, and potatoes wrapped in leeks
  and served with a delicious cucumber sauce.

Stuffed Pineapple $8.95
  Half pineapple stuffed with a medley of stir-fried vegetables.

Ravioli $9.95
  A blend of three cheeses—Ricotta, mozzarella, and provolone
  —fried mushrooms, spinach, and tomatoes stuffed in ravioli
  and covered with tomato and basil sauce.

Portobello Mushroom $9.95
  Grilled portebello mushroom served on a bed of vegetarian jambalaya.

(Continued on next page)

MENU C—ON MAIN STREET

Appetizers & Soups

House Salad. $2.95
Potato Skins. $4.95
Hot Chicken Wings $4.95
Steak Noodle Soup . . . . Cup $1.75
Bowl $3.25

Tomato Soup . . . . Cup $1.25
Bowl $2.75
New England
Clam Chowder. . . . . Cup $2.00
Bowl $3.75

From the Grill

Grilled Ham and Cheese Sandwich $5.95
*Melted American cheese over a slice of honey ham on sourdough bread.
Served with French fries and tomatoes.*

¼ lb. Grilled Hamburger on Bun $6.95
*¼ lb. of 100% beef grilled to order on an onion bun
with lettuce and tomato. Served with French fries.*

Pork Tenderloin Sandwich $5.95
*Tender slice of roasted pork tenderloin deep fried.
Served with glazed apple dressing.*

Grilled Chicken Breast Sandwich $7.95
*Broiled, boneless chicken breast hickory grilled over an open flame,
served with steamed vegetables.*

Homestyle Favorites

Italian Spaghetti $8.95
*Italian spaghetti with meat sauce or meatballs and two slices
of freshly baked garlic bread. Served with House Salad.*

Baked Chicken Dinner $6.95
*Baked chicken breast and thigh served with
baked potato and mixed vegetables.*

2. Log onto the USDA Web site or locate another diet analysis program. Using the food items listed on each menu in Step 1 and the information on the Web site or in the analysis program, complete the Food Intake Analysis chart that follows by:
   • Listing the amount of each food for each Healthy Eating Index (HEI) component.
   • Entering the amount recommended for each HEI component.
   • Adding up the HEI score and entering the total on the top line of the chart.

(Continued on next page)

Food Intake Analysis: Menu A—Just For Kids   **Total Score:**

Healthy Eating Index (HEI) Component	Score (Out of 10)	Portion Amount	Amount Recommended
Grain			
Vegetable			
Fruit			
Milk			
Meat			
HEI Component	Score (Out of 10)	Amount to Be Eaten	Amount Recommended
Total fat			
Saturated fat			
Cholesterol			
Sodium			
Variety			

Food Intake Analysis: Menu B—The Garden Spot   **Total Score:**

Healthy Eating Index (HEI) Component	Score (Out of 10)	Portion Amount	Amount Recommended
Grain			
Vegetable			
Fruit			
Milk			
Meat			
HEI Component	Score (Out of 10)	Amount to Be Eaten	Amount Recommended
Total fat			
Saturated fat			
Cholesterol			
Sodium			
Variety			

(Continued on next page)

Food Intake Analysis: Menu C—On the Menu			Total Score:
Healthy Eating Index (HEI) Component	Score (Out of 10)	Portion Amount	Amount Recommended
Grain			
Vegetable			
Fruit			
Milk			
Meat			
HEI Component	Score (Out of 10)	Amount to Be Eaten	Amount Recommended
Total fat			
Saturated fat			
Cholesterol			
Sodium			
Variety			

3. Based on the HEI score, how healthful is each menu?

   Menu A: _____

   Menu B: _____

   Menu C: _____

4. Review the foods listed in menus A, B, and C in Step 1. What changes need to be made to have a positive effect on the total HEI for each menu? Give alternative food items as needed to make each menu more nutritious.

   Menu A: _____

   Menu B: _____

   Menu C: _____

5. Revise the menus using these replacement food items. Continue to replace foods items until each menu achieves a 90–100 HEI score in the chart.

Researching Menu Types

Directions, Part 1 : Use Internet resources to research the types of menus listed below. Locate and print one example of each type of menu. You may want to use search engines, such as www.dogpile.com or www.snap.com for your research.

    A. Fixed menu   **C.** À la carte menu

    B. Cycle menu   **D.** Table d'hôte menu

Directions, Part 2 : Evaluate each menu for the following questions. Write your answers in the space provided. Use another sheet of paper and attach it to this activity sheet if necessary.

1. Who are the target customers for each menu?

    A. _____   **C.** _____

    B. _____   **D.** _____

2. What is the price range of each menu? How does this influence the target customers?

    A. _____   **C.** _____

    B. _____   **D.** _____

3. How do geography and culture influence each menu?

    A. _____

    B. _____

    C. _____

    D. _____

4. What eating trends are reflected in each menu?

    A. _____

    B. _____

    C. _____

    D. _____

Writing Menu Descriptions

Directions: In the charts that follow, write a menu description for each food item listed. Use the truth-in-menu guidelines in Chapter 12 for guidance. If you need more room, you may write your descriptions on a separate sheet of paper and attach it to this activity sheet.

Appetizer Menu Items	Description
Stuffed Mushrooms	
Potato Skins	

Soup Menu Items	Description
Steak-House Noodle Soup	
Onion Soup	

Salad Menu Items	Description
Cobb Salad	
Grilled Chicken Salad	

(Continued on next page)

Entrée Menu Items	Description
Surf and Turf	
Turkey and Dressing	

Accompaniment Menu Items	Description
Cheddar-Cheese Mashed Potatoes	
Broccoli-Cheese Casserole	

Dessert Menu Items	Description
Compote	
Apple Pie	

Beverage Menu Items	Description
Raspberry Lemonade	
Hot Chocolate	

Creating a Menu

Directions: Working in teams, select a type of restaurant and determine its menu items. Then create a menu by completing the steps that follow.

1. Select a type of restaurant from the list that follows:
   - Italian
   - Family dining
   - Submarine sandwich shop
   - Mexican
   - Asian
   - Coffee shop

2. Make a list of menu items for the type of restaurant your team selected. Be sure to include all traditional categories. List each menu item in the chart below.

3. Determine each menu item's selling price. Use the competitors' pricing method to determine the selling price by researching menu prices from at least three similar local restaurants. You also may use the Internet to find menus from a similar type of foodservice establishment. List each menu item's selling price in the chart below.

4. Write a menu description under each food item listed in the Menu Items chart.

5. Design a printed menu for your selected restaurant. Each menu must include the name of the restaurant, category headings, selling prices, menu selections with descriptions that follow truth-in-menu guidelines, and at least one illustration.

6. Print your menu. Menus may be generated by computer or by hand. Submit your team's finished menus for display.

Menu Items	
Menu Item and Description	**Selling Price**
1. Menu Item:	
Description:	
2. Menu Item:	
Description:	

(Continued on next page)

Menu Items, continued	
Menu Item and Description	**Selling Price**
3. Menu Item:	
Description:	
4. Menu Item:	
Description:	
5. Menu Item:	
Description:	
6. Menu Item:	
Description:	
7. Menu Item:	
Description:	
8. Menu Item:	
Description:	
9. Menu Item:	
Description:	
10. Menu Item:	
Description:	
11. Menu Item:	
Description:	
12. Menu Item:	
Description:	

Using Commercial Scales

Directions: Practice using each scale. Then demonstrate your skill for your instructor.

1. Demonstrate how to use a balance, portion, and electronic scale to weigh each of the items listed below.
   - 7 oz. granulated sugar
   - 1½ oz. salt
   - 2 lb. 2 oz. water
   - 3 lb. 4 oz. all-purpose flour

METHODS FOR USING SCALES

Portion Scale

1. Place the bowl on the platform.
2. Turn the dial until the needle is on zero.
3. Place the ingredient in the bowl.
4. Read the weight.

(Continued on next page)

Balance Scale

Method One:

1. Move the weight on the beam to zero.
2. Place the metal scoop on the left platform. Use this to weigh the ingredient.
3. Place the counterweight on the right platform. The counterweight is equal to the weight of the metal scoop on the left platform.
4. Move the weight on the beam to the desired weight.
5. Add the ingredient to the metal scoop until the beam is balanced.

Method Two:

1. Place a container large enough to hold the ingredient to be weighed on the left platform.
2. Move the bell-shaped weight on the beam to balance the scale.
3. Move the weight on the beam to the desired weight. Add any necessary individual weights to the right platform if desired weight is over 2 lbs.
4. Add the ingredient to the container on the left platform until the scale is balanced.

Electronic Scale Operation Sheet

1. Push the scale's power button.
2. Wait until the scale reads zero.
3. Place a light container on the scale.
4. Press the TARE button. It will subtract the container's weight. The scale will reset itself to read zero again.

5. Place the ingredient to be weighed in the container until the desired weight is reached. Remove the container.
6. Repeat Step 5 for each ingredient.
7. Turn off the scale.

Performance ✔ Checklist

Performance Standards

Level 4—Performs skill without supervision and adapts to problem situations.

Level 3—Performs skill satisfactorily without assistance or supervision.

Level 2—Performs skill satisfactorily, but requires assistance or supervision.

Level 1—Performs parts of skill satisfactorily, but requires considerable assistance or supervision.

Level 0—Cannot perform skill.

Attempt (circle one):   1   2   3   4

Comments: _____

_____

_____

_____

_____

_____

Performance Level Achieved: _____

_____ 1. Measures ingredients correctly.

_____ 2. Uses scales correctly.

Instructor's Signature: _____   **Date:** _____

Using a Standardized Formula

Directions: Working in teams, prepare chocolate chip cookies as directed by your instructor. Then evaluate each team's final product for quality and quantity. Answer the questions, and have your instructor complete the Performance Checklist that follows.

1. Did each team achieve the same quality and quantity? Why or why not?

_____

_____

2. What have you learned about standardized recipes and formulas?

_____

_____

_____

Performance ✔ Checklist

Performance Standards

Level 4—Performs skill without supervision and adapts to problem situations.

Level 3—Performs skill satisfactorily without assistance or supervision.

Level 2—Performs skill satisfactorily, but requires assistance or supervision.

Level 1—Performs parts of skill satisfactorily, but requires considerable assistance or supervision.

Level 0—Cannot perform skill.

Attempt (circle one):   1   2   3   4

Comments: _____

_____

_____

_____

_____

Performance Level Achieved: _____

_____ 1. Prepares ingredients as stated.

_____ 2. Softens fats correctly.

_____ 3. Adds sugars to creamed fats.

_____ 4. Adds dry ingredients in stages.

_____ 5. Uses appropriate mixing method.

_____ 6. Blends the dough well.

_____ 7. Portions the product appropriately.

_____ 8. Produces exact yield in formula.

Instructor's Signature: _____   **Date:** _____

Identifying Parts of a Recipe

Directions: Identify the parts of the recipe below. Write your answers in the space provided.

Southern Vegetable Soup ── 1

YIELD: 10 SERVINGS ── 2   SERVING SIZE: 8 OZ. ── 3

INGREDIENTS:

2 oz.	Salt pork, cut into small dice
10 oz.	Beef, bottom round, cut into small cubes
8 oz.	Canned peeled tomatoes, drained, seeded, and chopped
3½ qts.	Beef stock, heated to a boil
2 oz.	Frozen green beans
2 oz.	Red beans, cooked
4 oz.	Onions, peeled and diced brunoise
3 oz.	Celery stalks, washed, trimmed, and diced brunoise
6 oz.	Green cabbage, washed, cored, and chiffonade
3 oz.	Carrots, washed, peeled, and diced brunoise
2 oz.	Frozen corn kernels
2 oz.	Frozen okra, sliced
2 oz.	Zucchini, washed, trimmed, and cut in ½-in. dice
	Salt and freshly ground black pepper, to taste

── 4

METHOD OF PREPARATION:

1. In a large marmite, place the salt pork, and render the fat, stirring frequently until browned. Add the beef, reduce the heat, and sauté until browned.

2. Add the tomatoes, and sauté for another 2 minutes.

3. Add the boiling stock, and simmer until the meat is slightly firm in texture. ── 6

4. Add all other ingredients, and continue to simmer until vegetables are tender.

5. Season to taste and serve immediately in preheated cups, or hold at 140°F or higher. ── 7

── 5

1. _____   5. _____

2. _____   6. _____

3. _____   7. _____

4. _____

Converting a Recipe #1

Directions: Convert the recipe for *Omelet with Cheese* that follows by using the "Total Yield Conversion Method." Use the steps that follow.

Omelet with Cheese

YIELD: 10 SERVINGS   SERVING SIZE: 8 OZ.

INGREDIENTS:

30	Eggs, cracked into a bowl
	Salt and ground white pepper, to taste
8 oz.	Milk
5 oz.	Clarified butter, melted
3 oz.	Fresh parsley, washed, excess moisture removed, and chopped
1 lb.	Cheese, **julienne**

METHOD OF PREPARATION:

1. Season the eggs with salt and pepper. Add the milk, and **whisk** until the eggs are well combined.

2. Heat an omelet pan with ½ oz. of butter.

3. When hot, add a 6-oz. ladle of egg mixture.

4. Shake the pan, and mix the eggs until they begin to firm, lifting the edges to allow liquid egg to run underneath (see chef notes).

5. When the omelet is almost firm, or 145°F, turn it over.

6. Place the cheese in the center of the omelet, fold, and roll onto a preheated dinner plate. Serve immediately, or hold at 140°F.

7. Repeat the procedure until all of the eggs are cooked.

8. Garnish with chopped parsley.

(Continued on next page)

1. Use the following formula to determine the conversion factor. The desired yield of the recipe is 25 servings:

   desired yield ÷ existing yield = conversion factor

2. Use the Conversion Form below to calculate the conversion for each ingredient listed in the recipe. Answer the questions that follow. You may use Chapter 13 as a guide for recipe conversions.

Conversion Form

Standardized recipe name: _____

Existing serving yield: _____   Converted serving yield: _____

Ingredient	Amount	Multiplied By	Conversion Factor	Equals	New Yield
Eggs	30	×		=	
Milk	8 oz.	×		=	
Clarified butter	5 oz.	×		=	
Fresh parsley	3 oz.	×		=	
Cheese	1 lb.	×		=	

A. What changes may need to be made to the cooking time?

_____

_____

B. What changes may need to be made to the cooking temperature?

_____

_____

C. What equipment changes may need to be made?

_____

_____

Converting a Recipe #2

Directions: Select a standardized recipe. Then complete the steps that follow.

1. Use the following formula to increase the yield of the recipe by 15 servings:
   Step A desired yield ÷ existing yield = conversion factor
   Step B existing quantity × conversion factor = desired quantity

2. Calculate the number of servings you would get from the recipe if the portion size is doubled. Use the following formula:
   Step A existing portions × existing portion size = total existing yield
   Step B desired portions × desired portion size = new yield
   Step C new yield ÷ existing yield = conversion factor
   Step D existing yield × conversion factor = new yield

   Record your calculations and answers in the space below. You may use a separate sheet of paper if necessary.

(Continued on next page)

3. Use the Conversion Form below to calculate the conversion for each ingredient listed in the recipe. Answer the questions that follow. You may use Chapter 13 as a guide for recipe conversions.

Conversion Form

Standardized recipe name: _____

Existing serving yield: _____   Converted serving yield: _____

Ingredient	Amount	Multiplied By	Conversion Factor	Equals	New Yield
		×		=	
		×		=	
		×		=	
		×		=	
		×		=	
		×		=	
		×		=	
		×		=	
		×		=	
		×		=	

Standardized pan size: _____   Converted pan size: _____

Standardized serving size: _____   Converted serving size: _____

A. What changes need to be made to the cooking time?

_____

B. What changes need to be made to the cooking temperature?

_____

C. What equipment changes need to be made?

_____

Culinary Essentials Lab Manual
Copyright © Glencoe/McGraw-Hill

Calculating Food Costs

Directions: Calculate food costs for selected food items. Determine raw yield percentages. Complete the steps that follow:

1. Complete the Unit Cost worksheet below by calculating the unit price for each ingredient and recording the results.

Unit Cost		
Food Product	**As-Purchased Price**	**Unit Price**
Stewed tomatoes	29 oz./$0.95	/ oz.
Carrots	1 lb./$0.95	/ oz.
Apples	6 lbs./$7.85	/ oz.
Celery	1 lb./$ 1.25	/ oz.
Oranges	1 lb./$0.89	/ oz.
Shredded cheese	5 lbs./$10.25	/ oz.
Milk	1 gallon/$2.29	/ fl. oz.
Cake flour	50 lbs./$34.95	/ oz.
Turkey breast, cooked	15 lbs./$44.95	/ oz.
Onions, whole fresh	12 lbs./$10.98	/ oz.
Boneless beef roast	1 lb./$3.75	/ oz.
Boneless chicken breast	1 lb./$2.89	/ oz.
Chicken breast, w/bones	1 lb./$1.79	/ oz.
Beef stew, 2" cubed	10 lb./$28.90	/ oz.
Cabbage	50 lb./$34.95	/ oz.
Bananas	4 lb./$0.79	/ oz.
Cream of mushroom soup	3¼ lbs./$2.75	/ oz.

(Continued on next page)

2. Perform a raw yield test. Choose one or more of the foods from the Raw Yield Percentage chart on the next page. Complete the steps that follow and record your results on the Raw Yield Percentage chart.

   a. Weigh the food product on a food scale to get the AP (as purchased) weight. Record this AP Weight.

   b. Clean the food products, and trim off, any unusable parts.

   c. Weigh the unusable parts, or trim loss. Record in the Trim Loss Weight.

   d. Using the formula below, subtract the **trim loss weight** from the **AP weight** to find the **yield weight**. Show your calculations in the space provided. Then record the Yield Weight.

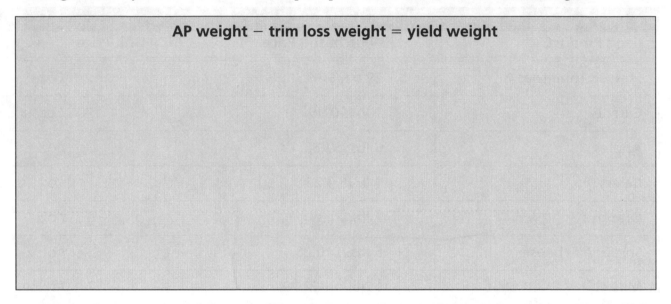

AP weight − trim loss weight = yield weight

   e. Using the formula below, divide the **Y weight** by the **AP weight** to find a **yield percentage**. Show your calculations in the space provided. Then record the Yield Percentage.

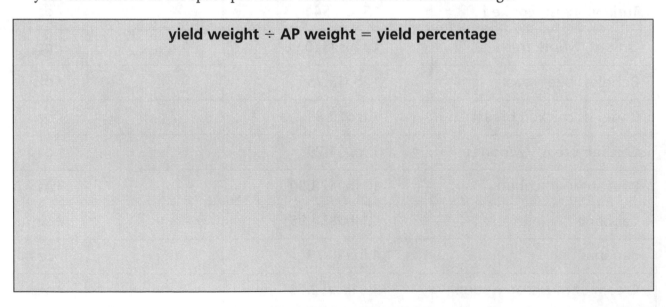

yield weight ÷ AP weight = yield percentage

(Continued on next page)

Culinary Essentials Lab Manual
Copyright © Glencoe/McGraw-Hill

Raw Yield Percentage					
Item	Amount	AP Weight	Trim Loss Weight	Yield Weight	Yield Percentage
Carrots	10				
Apples	4				
Celery	1 bunch				
Oranges	4				
Cabbage	1 head				
Bananas	4				
Onions	4 medium				
Green peppers	2				

Recipe Costing

Directions: Select a recipe from those provided by your instructor. Then use the Recipe Costing form below to cost out the recipe. Use the information on page 320 of your text as a guide. Ask your instructor for current as-purchased (AP) and Q-factor amounts. Then determine the cost per portion.

A. Recipe Name: _____ **C. Yield:** _____

B. Portion Size: _____ **D. Menu Category:** _____

E. Ingredient		F. EP%	G. AP Amount	H. Unit Purchase Price		I. Cost per Unit	J. Ingredient Cost
Quantity	Item	EP%	Quantity	Cost	Unit		
	K. Ingredient Cost Total						
	L. Q Factor (5%)						
	M. Total Recipe Cost						
	N. Portion Cost						

How Cooking Alters Food

Directions: Working in teams, explore the Mallaird reaction and how cooking affects food. Complete the steps that follow.

1. Choose three food items from the following. List your selections in the chart below.

   - Mushrooms
   - Pears
   - Chicken
   - Apples
   - Broccoli
   - Pork chops
   - Onions
   - Ham
   - Carrots
   - Fish
   - Peppers
   - Sirloin tips

2. Place a small amount of oil in a shallow pan or wok.

3. Heat the pan until you see ripples in the oil.

4. Add one food item to the pan. Note your start time, and mark this on the chart below.

5. Cook the food item until it browns, observing the browning process. Note the stop time, and mark this in the chart below.

6. Repeat steps 4 and 5 using a different food item and complete the chart.

	Food Item	Sugar Added	Level of Browning	Start Time	Stop Time
A.					
B.					
C.					

7. Evaluate each food item to determine how cooking affected the finished product. What happened to the color of each food item? What was the crust like? Describe the texture. How did the aroma change? Describe the flavor. Record your observations in the charts on the next page.

8. Describe how the information you gathered about the Maillard reaction could impact customer orders.

_____

_____

_____

(Continued on next page)

Product Assessment: Item A	
Color	
Crust	
Texture	
Aroma	
Flavor	

Product Assessment: Item B	
Color	
Crust	
Texture	
Aroma	
Flavor	

Product Assessment: Item C	
Color	
Crust	
Texture	
Aroma	
Flavor	

Moist Cooking

Directions: Working in teams, practice using moist cooking techniques needed to prepare Tomato Concassé.

1. Gather a 1-qt. saucepan, a 1-qt. bowl of ice water, a tomato, a slotted spoon, a paring knife, a chef's knife, and a cutting board.

2. Set the saucepan on the burner. Rinse the tomato. Place the tomato in the saucepan. Fill the saucepan with enough water to cover the tomato.

3. Remove the tomato. Let the water begin to heat until it comes to a simmer.

4. Remove the stem and cut an "X" at the bottom of the tomato.

5. Put the tomato in the saucepan. Blanch the tomato for 15–30 seconds.

6. Remove the tomato from the simmering water.

7. Plunge the tomato into the ice water. This is the shocking process.

8. Remove the skin from the tomato.

9. Cut the tomato in half.

10. Squeeze out the seeds, and dice the tomato. This is the final product, which may be used as is.

11. Team members should sample the finished product.

Performance ✔ Checklist

Performance Standards	Attempt (circle one): 1 2 3 4
Level 4—Performs skill without supervision and adapts to problem situations.	Comments: _____
Level 3—Performs skill satisfactorily without assistance or supervision.	_____
Level 2—Performs skill satisfactorily, but requires assistance or supervision.	_____
Level 1—Performs parts of skill satisfactorily, but requires considerable assistance or supervision.	_____
Level 0—Cannot perform skill.	Performance Level Achieved: _____

_____ 1. Performs simmering, blanching, and shocking correctly.

_____ 2. Performs safety and sanitation practices at all times during this job.

Instructor's Signature: _____ **Date:** _____

Combination Cooking

Directions: Working in teams, practice using a combination cooking technique by braising vegetables. Complete the steps that follow.

1. Gather a frying or roasting pan, fat, a mirepoix, a liquid, and raw celery, carrots, and potatoes.

2. Heat the fat in the pan. Add the mirepoix and heat briefly.

3. Wash and dice the vegetables. Place the vegetables in the pan and sear them.

4. Remove the vegetables from the pan and deglaze the pan.

5. Return the vegetables to the deglazed pan. Add enough liquid, such as water or stock, to the pan of vegetables to partly cover them.

6. Cover the pan and place it into a preheated 350°F oven. Cook the food slowly until it is fork tender.

7. Team members should sample the finished product.

Performance ✔ Checklist

Performance Standards

Level 4—Performs skill without supervision and adapts to problem situations.

Level 3—Performs skill satisfactorily without assistance or supervision.

Level 2—Performs skill satisfactorily, but requires assistance or supervision.

Level 1—Performs parts of skill satisfactorily, but requires considerable assistance or supervision.

Level 0—Cannot perform skill.

Attempt (circle one):   1   2   3   4

Comments: _____

_____

_____

_____

_____

Performance Level Achieved: _____

_____ 1. All team members are ready and perform mise en place effectively.

_____ 2. Performs safety and sanitation practices at all times during this job.

_____ 3. Performs braising correctly.

Instructor's Signature: _____ Date: _____

Identifying Herbs & Spices

Directions: Smell the aroma of each of the herbs and spices in the numbered cups provided by your instructor. Identify each one by name and describe its key characteristics. Mark your responses in the chart that follows.

Herb or Spice	Description
1.	
2.	
3.	
4.	
5.	
6.	
7.	
8.	
9.	

(Continued on next page)

Herb or Spice	Description
10.	
11.	
12.	
13.	
14.	
15.	
16.	
17.	
18.	
19.	
20.	

(Continued on next page)

Culinary Essentials Lab Manual
Copyright © Glencoe/McGraw-Hill

Herb or Spice	Description
21.	
22.	
23.	
24.	
25.	
26.	
27.	
28.	
29.	
30.	

Using Herbs & Spices

Directions: Work in teams. Practice using herbs and spices by completing the steps that follow.

Part A—Flavoring Soup

1. Select five fresh herbs and whole spices that can be used in soup.

2. Heat chicken broth for 10 people. Separate the broth into five smaller batches.

3. Add salt and one herb or spice to each batch.

4. Taste-test each batch.

5. Record your results in the chart below.

Batch	Herb or Spice	Flavor of Soup
A		
B		
C		
D		
E		

Part B—Flavoring Potatoes

1. Boil 5 potatoes.

2. Separate the potatoes into five small batches.

3. Select and add one herb or spice to each batch.

4. Taste-test each batch.

5. Record your results in the chart below.

Batch	Herb or Spice	Flavor of Potatoes
A		
B		
C		
D		
E		

Linking Taste & Smell

Directions: Working in teams, take turns tasting a variety of food items. Then complete the charts that follow.

Part A:

1. Gather 2 apples and 2 potatoes. Peel the skins from both.

2. Cut the apples and potatoes into quarters. Keep the shapes the same.

3. Put the apple and potato slices in separate bowls. Set them aside.

4. Close your eyes and pinch your nose shut.

5. Have a team member randomly hand you an item from each of the bowls. Take a bite of each food item. Which was the apple? Which was the potato? Are both tastes unknown?

6. Unpinch your nose, but keep your eyes closed. Taste each food item again. Which was the apple? Which was the potato?

7. Repeat steps 4–6 until each team member has taken a turn.

8. In the chart below, indicate by tally marks which item each team member tasted in each trial.

Taste Trial	Apple	Potato	Unknown
Nose pinched shut			
Nose not pinched			

(Continued on next page)

Part B:

1. Gather 8 wooden craft sticks, two plastic cups, vinegar, and sugar.

2. Pour a small amount of vinegar and a small amount of sugar into each plastic cup.

3. Close your eyes and pinch your nose shut.

4. Dip one craft stick into the vinegar and one craft stick into the sugar.

5. Touch the vinegar-soaked end of the stick to the tip of your tongue. What did you taste?

6. Rinse your mouth with water.

7. Touch the craft stick with sugar to your tongue. What did you taste? Rinse your mouth.

8. Unpinch your nose, but keep your eyes closed. Touch each craft stick to the tip of your tongue a second time, rinsing between each one. What did you taste?

9. Repeat steps 3-8 until each team member has taken a turn.

10. In the chart below, indicate by tally marks which item each team member tasted in each trial.

Taste Trial	Vinegar	Sugar	Unknown
Nose pinched shut			
Nose not pinched			

Part C:

1. What does this experiment tell you about the link between taste and smell?

_____

_____

_____

_____

_____

_____

_____

Culinary Essentials Lab Manual
Copyright © Glencoe/McGraw-Hill

Cooking Breakfast Meats

Directions: Working in teams, prepare breakfast meats by completing the steps that follow.

1. In the charts that follow, write the cooking procedure for each breakfast meat listed.

Ham	
Step 1	
Step 2	
Step 3	

Bacon	
Step 1	
Step 2	
Step 3	
Step 4	
Step 5	
Step 6	

Sausage	
Step 1	
Step 2	
Step 3	
Step 4	
Step 5	

(Continued on next page)

2. Following the procedures outlined in your charts, cook each of the breakfast meats.

3. Plate each cooked breakfast meat.

4. Taste each finished product, then answer the questions that follow:

   a. How did the ham taste? Was it cooked properly?

   _____

   _____

   _____

   b. How much less did the bacon weigh after it had been cooked? Why?

   _____

   _____

   _____

   c. How did the bacon taste? Was it thoroughly cooked? Greasy?

   _____

   _____

   _____

   d. Which breakfast meat was the most difficult to cook? Explain why.

   _____

   _____

   _____

   e. Which breakfast meat was the easiest to prepare? Explain why.

   _____

   _____

   _____

   _____

   _____

(Continued on next page)

5. Present plated samples of each cooked breakfast meat. Have your instructor complete the Performance Checklist.

Performance ✔ Checklist

Performance Standards	**Attempt (circle one):** 1 2 3 4
Level 4—Performs skill without supervision and adapts to problem situations.	Comments: _____
Level 3—Performs skill satisfactorily without assistance or supervision.	_____
Level 2—Performs skill satisfactorily, but requires assistance or supervision.	_____
Level 1—Performs parts of skill satisfactorily, but requires considerable assistance or supervision.	_____
Level 0—Cannot perform skill.	**Performance Level Achieved:** _____

_____ 1. Follows safety and sanitation practices at all times during this job.

_____ 2. Browns and cooks the ham to an internal temperature of 145°F for 15 seconds.

_____ 3. Neatly slices and attractively plates the ham.

_____ 4. Prepares ham to the proper flavor, texture, doneness, and appearance.

_____ 5. Cooks the bacon in the oven or on the griddle and to an internal temperature of 145°F for 15 seconds.

_____ 6. Attractively plates the bacon.

_____ 7. Prepares the bacon to proper flavor, texture, doneness, and appearance.

_____ 8. Cooks the sausage in the oven or on the griddle to an internal temperature of 155°F for 15 seconds.

_____ 9. The sausage was finished on the griddle, using the appropriate temperature.

_____ 10. Attractively plates the sausage.

_____ 11. Prepares the sausage to proper flavor, texture, doneness, and appearance.

Instructor's Signature: _____ **Date:** _____

Preparing Baked Ham

Directions: Working in teams, prepare baked ham by following the recipe below.

COOKING TECHNIQUE:
Bake

Bake:
1. Preheat the oven.
2. Place the food product on the appropriate rack.

HACCP:
Hold at 140°F or above.

HAZARDOUS FOOD:
Ham

NUTRITION:
Calories: 82.6
Fat: 5.71 g
Protein: 7.34 g

Baked Ham Slices

YIELD: 50 SERVINGS   SERVING SIZE: 1½ OZ.

INGREDIENTS:

5 lbs.   Ham, fully-cooked, boneless, trimmed of fat

METHOD OF PREPARATION:

1. Preheat the broiler or oven to 350°F.

2. Slice the ham into 1½-oz. portions, and lay out on sheet pans.

3. Bake to an internal temperature of 145°F, about 10 minutes. Remove, and transfer to hotel pans for service. Hold at 140°F or above.

Performance ✔ Checklist

Performance Standards

Level 4—Performs skill without supervision and adapts to problem situations.

Level 3—Performs skill satisfactorily without assistance or supervision.

Level 2—Performs skill satisfactorily, but requires assistance or supervision.

Level 1—Performs parts of skill satisfactorily, but requires considerable assistance or supervision.

Level 0—Cannot perform skill.

Attempt (circle one):   1   2   3   4

Comments: _____

_____

_____

_____

_____

_____

Performance Level Achieved: _____

_____ 1. Follows safety and sanitation practices at all times during this job.

_____ 2. Browns and cooks the ham to an internal temperature of 145°F for 15 seconds.

_____ 3. Neatly slices and attractively plates the ham.

_____ 4. Prepares the final product to proper flavor, texture, doneness, and appearance.

Instructor's Signature: _____ **Date:** _____

Cooking Eggs

Directions: Work in teams to cook eggs. Complete the steps that follow.

1. In the charts that follow, write the cooking procedure for each type of egg listed.

Fried Eggs (sunny-side up)	
Step 1	
Step 2	
Step 3	
Step 4	

Fried Eggs (basted)	
Step 1	
Step 2	
Step 3	
Step 4	

Fried Eggs (over easy)	
Step 1	
Step 2	
Step 3	
Step 4	

(Continued on next page)

Fried Eggs (over medium)	
Step 1	
Step 2	
Step 3	
Step 4	

Fried Eggs (over hard)	
Step 1	
Step 2	
Step 3	
Step 4	

Scrambled Eggs	
Step 1	
Step 2	
Step 3	
Step 4	
Step 5	
Step 6	

Poached Eggs	
Step 1	
Step 2	
Step 3	
Step 4	
Step 5	

(Continued on next page)

Shirred Eggs

Step 1	
Step 2	
Step 3	
Step 4	
Step 5	
Step 6	
Step 7	
Step 8	

Eggs Simmered in the Shell

Step 1	
Step 2	
Step 3	
Step 4	

American Omelets

Step 1	
Step 2	
Step 3	
Step 4	
Step 5	
Step 6	
Step 7	

(Continued on next page)

2. Following the procedures listed in the charts above, cook each type of egg. Use egg rings to cook at least two types of fried eggs.

3. Plate each type of cooked egg.

4. Present plated samples of each cooked egg type to your instructor for evaluation. Have the Performance Checklist completed.

Performance ✔ Checklist

Performance Standards

Level 4—Performs skill without supervision and adapts to problem situations.

Level 3—Performs skill satisfactorily without assistance or supervision.

Level 2—Performs skill satisfactorily, but requires assistance or supervision.

Level 1—Performs parts of skill satisfactorily, but requires considerable assistance or supervision.

Level 0—Cannot perform skill.

Attempt (circle one): 1 2 3 4

Comments: _____

_____

_____

_____

_____

Performance Level Achieved: _____

_____ 1. Follows safety and sanitation practices at all times during this job.

_____ 2. Uses the correct grade of egg.

_____ 3. The yolk of the sunny-side-up egg is visible, highly mounded, and yellow.

_____ 4. The yolk of the basted egg has a thin cover of white over it.

_____ 5. The yolk of the egg cooked over easy is yellow and runny.

_____ 6. The yolk of the egg cooked over medium is yellow and partly cooked.

_____ 7. The yolk of the egg cooked over hard is yellow, fully cooked, and firm.

_____ 8. The eggs cooked in the egg rings are uniform in shape.

_____ 9. The scrambled eggs are properly coagulated and are not curdled.

_____ 10. The poached egg is tender.

_____ 11. The shirred egg is cooked properly and garnished artistically.

_____ 12. Each type of simmered egg is cooked the proper length of time, producing desired results.

_____ 13. The American omelet is light and puffy.

_____ 14. Prepares all egg dishes to appropriate flavor, texture, doneness, and appearance.

Instructor's Signature: _____ **Date:** _____

Breakfast Production

Directions: Working in teams, prepare multiple breakfast orders. Complete the steps that follow.

1. Review these breakfast orders.
   a. Pancakes and sausage.
   b. Two fried eggs over easy with hash browns and a side of wheat toast.
   c. Oatmeal with a side of raisin toast.
   d. Cheese omelet, bacon, country-fried potatoes, and a side of white toast. Use the Omelet with Cheese recipe on page 107 of this activity.
   e. French toast with ham with two scrambled eggs.

2. In the space below, list the ingredients you will need to cook all five orders. Then gather the supplies.

Ingredient	Amount

(Continued on next page)

3. Fill in the task and the start time of each task on the Production Schedule on this page.

4. Following your production schedule, cook the breakfast orders. Complete the Production Schedule by filling in the stop time for each task.

Production Schedule		
Task	Start Time	Stop Time

(Continued on next page)

COOKING TECHNIQUE:
Shallow-Fry

Shallow-Fry:
1. Heat the cooking medium to the proper temperature.
2. Cook the food product throughout.
3. Season, and serve hot.

GLOSSARY:
Whisk: to aerate with a whip
Julienne: cut into ⅛-in. strips

HACCP:

Cook to 145°F.
Hold cooked eggs at 140°F or above.
Hold uncooked egg mixture 41°F or below.

HAZARDOUS FOODS:
Eggs
Milk

NUTRITION:
Calories: 506
Fat: 41.9 g
Protein: 28.9 g

CHEF NOTE:
When the eggs have set in the sauté pan, place the pan under a broiler for 10–15 seconds to finish cooking the eggs; then roll the omelet out of the pan and onto a preheated serving plate. This creates a fluffier presentation and ensures that the eggs are well done.

Omelet with Cheese

YIELD: 10 SERVINGS   SERVING SIZE: 8 OZ.

INGREDIENTS:

30	Eggs, cracked into a bowl
	Salt and ground white pepper, to taste
8 oz.	Milk
5 oz.	Clarified butter, melted
3 oz.	Fresh parsley, washed, excess moisture removed, and chopped
1 lb.	Cheese, **julienne**

METHOD OF PREPARATION:

1. Season the eggs with salt and pepper. Add the milk, and **whisk** until the eggs are well combined.

2. Heat an omelet pan with ½ oz. of butter.

3. When hot, add a 6-oz. ladle of egg mixture.

4. Shake the pan, and mix the eggs until they begin to firm, lifting the edges to allow liquid egg to run underneath (see chef note).

5. When the omelet is almost firm, or 145°F, turn it over.

6. Place the cheese in the center of the omelet, fold, and roll onto a preheated dinner plate. Serve immediately, or hold at 140°F or above.

7. Repeat the procedure until all of the eggs are cooked.

8. Garnish with chopped parsley.

(Continued on next page)

5. Present each plated breakfast order to your instructor for evaluation, and have the Performance Checklist below completed.

Performance ✔ Checklist

Performance Standards	
Level 4—Performs skill without supervision and adapts to problem situations.	**Attempt (circle one):** 1 2 3 4
Level 3—Performs skill satisfactorily without assistance or supervision.	Comments: _____
Level 2—Performs skill satisfactorily, but requires assistance or supervision.	_____
Level 1—Performs parts of skill satisfactorily, but requires considerable assistance or supervision.	_____
Level 0—Cannot perform skill.	**Performance Level Achieved:** _____

_____ 1. Follows safety and sanitation practices at all times during this job.

_____ 2. Plans and gathers all equipment and ingredients before beginning.

_____ 3. Completes the Production Schedule professionally.

_____ 4. Times each food order to be ready at the same time.

_____ 5. Food orders are ready at the same time.

_____ 6. The breakfast meats are thoroughly cooked to the following internal temperatures: bacon—145°F for 15 seconds; ham—145°F for 15 seconds; sausage—155°F for 15 seconds.

_____ 7. The scrambled eggs and omelet are properly coagulated, not overcooked or undercooked, and are cooked to an internal temperature of 145°F for 15 seconds.

_____ 8. The yolk of the egg cooked over easy is yellow and runny with a thin white covering.

_____ 9. The potatoes are cooked to tenderness, nicely browned, and hot.

_____ 10. The pancakes and French toast are tender.

_____ 11. The toast is light and crisp, not overly dry or soggy.

_____ 12. The oatmeal is served at the correct consistency and with appropriate accompaniments.

_____ 13. Prepares all breakfast foods to proper flavor, texture, doneness, and appearance.

Instructor's Signature: _____   **Date:** _____

Identifying Garnishing Tools

Directions: Identify each garnishing tool. Write the name below the photo. Then, in the space beside the photo, describe the technique used with each tool to prepare a decorative garnish.

_____
_____
_____
_____
_____

1. _____

_____
_____
_____
_____
_____

2. _____

_____
_____
_____
_____

3. _____

_____
_____
_____
_____
_____

4. _____

(Continued on next page)

5. _____

6. _____

7. _____

8. _____

Creating Apple Bird Garnishes

Directions: Create apple bird garnishes using the directions that follow. Once you have completed your garnishes, have your instructor complete the performance evaluation.

1. Gather a large, fresh apple, such as a Red or Golden Delicious apple, a cutting board, a paring knife, a bowl of water mixed with lemon juice, and two whole cloves.
2. Create a base for your apple bird by cutting about ⅓ of the apple off from the side of the apple. Save the small piece of apple to use for the head and neck of the bird.
3. Dip the cut portions of the apple into water and lemon juice to prevent browning.
4. With the stem end of the apple facing you, put the cut side of the apple down on a flat surface.
5. Using a paring knife, cut a small, "V-shaped" wedge from the top side of the apple. Set the wedge aside.
6. To cut a series of top feathers, continue cutting V-shaped wedges from the top of the apple, about ⅛-in. thick, until you have a series of five to seven wedges. You may need to switch to a larger knife as the wedges get larger. Put the cut wedges into the bowl with water and lemon juice to prevent browning while you work.
7. To cut a series of side feathers, cut V-shaped wedges from both sides of the apple repeating the directions followed in step 6. Keep the wedges from each side of the apple together to form the wing feathers in step 10. Be sure to place the wedges in the lemon juice, and dip the apple in the lemon juice, too.
8. Place the base of the apple on a flat surface.

Step 2: Creating a base.

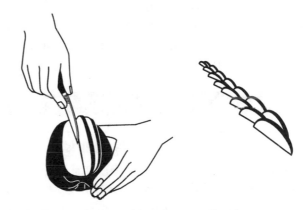

Step 6: Cutting wedges for top feathers.

Step 7: Cutting wedges for side feathers.

(Continued on next page)

9. To put together the top feathers, start with the largest wedge from the top of the apple. Put this wedge into the top wedge cut, about ⅓ of the way toward the back of the apple. Then, take the next smallest wedge and put it into the previous wedge, extending it as you did the first wedge. Repeat until you have placed all of the wedges for the top feathers. The top feathers should extend off the back of the bird.

10. To put together the wing feathers, repeat the procedure followed in step 9.

11. Using the piece of apple saved from the base in step 2, cut about a ¼-in. strip from the center of this piece of apple to make the head and neck of the bird. Insert the whole cloves on either side of the head to form the bird's eyes.

12. Insert the head and neck in the wedge toward the stem-end of the apple.

13. Pour some of the water and lemon juice over your bird once you have it put together.

14. Display your completed bird.

Steps 9 & 10: Placing the top and side feathers.

Step 14: Finished bird.

Performance ✔ Checklist

Performance Standards	
Level 4—Performs skill without supervision and adapts to problem situations.	**Attempt (circle one):** 1 2 3 4
Level 3—Performs skill satisfactorily without assistance or supervision.	Comments: _____
Level 2—Performs skill satisfactorily, but requires assistance or supervision.	_____
Level 1—Performs parts of skill satisfactorily, but requires considerable assistance or supervision.	_____
Level 0—Cannot perform skill.	_____
	PERFORMANCE LEVEL ACHIEVED: _____

_____ 1. Follows safety and sanitation practices at all times during this job.

_____ 2. Follows the procedures for making garnishes accurately.

_____ 3. Displays garnishes neatly and attractively.

Instructor's Signature: _____ **Date:** _____

Creating Flower Garnishes

Directions: Create flower garnishes using the directions that follow. Once you have completed your garnishes, have your instructor complete the performance evaluation.

Lily

1. Gather the following vegetables and equipment: turnips, beets, or rutabagas at least 3 inches in diameter, carrot or lemon, a mandoline, paring knife or zester, and wooden toothpicks.
2. Wash and trim the ends of the vegetables.
3. Make paper-thin slices of the vegetables (except the carrot) using a mandoline.
4. Cut julienne strips of the carrot, or cut several strips of lemon zest to form the stamens of the lilies.
5. Roll the first vegetable slice tightly around a strip of carrot or lemon zest. Hold at the base.
6. While tightly holding the base of the lily center, loosely wrap the bottom of another vegetable slice around the base of the lily, opposite the previous slice to form the petals.
7. Continue wrapping 3 to 5 vegetable slices around the lily. Fasten at the base using toothpicks.
8. Chill in ice water until the lily petals are firm. Use as needed to garnish plates.
9. Refrigerate unused lilies in a tightly-sealed container until needed.

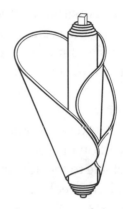

Step 4: Rolling the center of the lily.

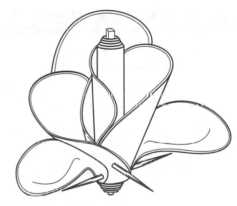

Step 5: Making lily petals.

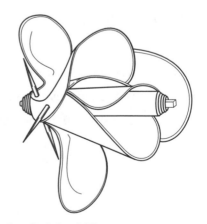

Step 6: The finished lily.

(Continued on next page)

Scallion/Leek Flower

1. Gather a paring knife, cutting board, and several scallions or leeks.
2. Cut the scallion or leek about 2–3 inches from the root end, removing the entire darker green portion.
3. Cut off the roots without removing the root ends from either the scallion or leek.
4. Make vertical slices into the scallion or leek, being careful not to cut through the root end. Make the slices very close together all around the scallion or leek.
5. Insert a small skewer or toothpick into the root end of the scallion or leek.
6. Spin the vegetable to separate the flower petals.
7. Chill the scallion or leek in ice water to set the petals.

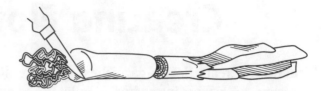

Step 2: Paring the scallion or leek.

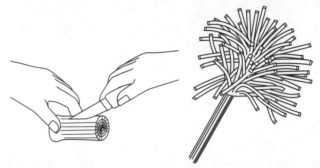

Step 4: Making vertical slices.

Step 6: Separating the flower petals.

Performance ✔ Checklist

Performance Standards
Level 4—Performs skill without supervision and adapts to problem situations.
Level 3—Performs skill satisfactorily without assistance or supervision.
Level 2—Performs skill satisfactorily, but requires assistance or supervision.
Level 1—Performs parts of skill satisfactorily, but requires considerable assistance or supervision.
Level 0—Cannot perform skill.

Attempt (circle one): 1   2   3   4

Comments: _____

_____

_____

_____

_____

_____

Performance Level Achieved: _____

_____ 1. Follows safety and sanitation practices at all times during this job.

_____ 2. Follows the procedures for making garnishes accurately.

_____ 3. Displays garnishes neatly and attractively.

Instructor's Signature: _____ **Date:** _____

Salads & Dressings

Directions: Working in teams, prepare one type of salad and three types of salad dressing. Use the recipes provided by your instructor. Complete the steps that follow.

Part A

1. Select a salad type from this list:
   - Appetizer salad
   - Accompaniment salad
   - Main-course salad
   - Separate-course salad
   - Dessert salad

2. Obtain a recipe from your instructor. Review the recipe, noting what ingredients you will need.

3. Complete the Job Plan Sheet. Submit it to your instructor for approval before proceeding.

4. Prepare your salad following your recipe and your approved Job Plan Sheet.

5. After your salad is done, store it while you prepare the salad dressings.

Job Plan Sheet

Salad type: _____

Recipe: _____

Yield: _____   **Portion size:** _____

Ingredient:	Amount:	Ingredient:	Amount:
_____	_____	_____	_____
_____	_____	_____	_____
_____	_____	_____	_____
_____	_____	_____	_____
_____	_____	_____	_____

Equipment:	Use:	Equipment:	Use:
_____	_____	_____	_____
_____	_____	_____	_____
_____	_____	_____	_____

(Continued on next page)

List each step in the preparation process below.

_____

_____

_____

_____

_____

_____

_____

_____

_____

_____

Write any special instructions:

_____

_____

_____

_____

List any suggested salad dressing:

_____

_____

_____

_____

Part B

1. Obtain three salad dressing recipes from your instructor: a vinaigrette dressing, a fatty dressing, and a cooked dressing. Review each recipe.

2. In the charts on page 117, list the procedure used to make each type of salad dressing.

(Continued on next page)

Vinaigrette Dressing Procedure	
Step 1	
Step 2	
Step 3	

Fatty Dressing Procedure	
Step 1	
Step 2	
Step 3	

Cooked Dressing Procedure	
Step 1	
Step 2	
Step 3	
Step 4	
Step 5	

3. Prepare each type of salad dressing, following your recipes and procedures in step 2.

Part C

1. Bring out your salad and set it beside your three prepared salad dressings.

2. Determine which, if any, of your prepared salad dressings would complement your salad.

3. Add your salad dressing to your salad, if appropriate, and present it to your instructor for evaluation.

(Continued on next page)

Performance ✔ Checklist

<table>
<tr><td>

Performance Standards

Level 4—Performs skill without supervision and adapts to problem situations.

Level 3—Performs skill satisfactorily without assistance or supervision.

Level 2—Performs skill satisfactorily, but requires assistance or supervision.

Level 1—Performs parts of skill satisfactorily, but requires considerable assistance or supervision.

Level 0—Cannot perform skill.

</td><td>

Attempt (circle one):　1　2　3　4

Comments: _____

_____

_____

_____

_____

_____

Performance Level Achieved: _____

</td></tr>
</table>

_____　1. Follows safety and sanitation practices at all times during this job.

_____　2. Completes the Job Plan Sheet in a thorough and professional manner.

_____　3. Follows the proper vinaigrette dressing procedure.

_____　4. Follows the proper fatty dressing procedure.

_____　5. Follows the proper cooked dressing procedure.

_____　6. Follows recipes to produce quality dressings.

_____　7. Achieves the proper consistency in all dressings.

_____　8. The dressings are flavorful.

_____　9. The salads are structured correctly.

_____　10. The salads are correctly plated and attractively garnished.

Instructor's Signature: _____　**Date:** _____

Cold Food Buffet

Directions: Plan presentation platters and buffet table layouts by completing the steps that follow.

1. Plan a buffet menu that consists of five of the following cold food platters: hors d'oeuvres, canapés, crudités, fancy sandwiches, antipasto, cheese, meat, fruit, or a combination of cold foods. Take into account the ingredients, colors, textures, and preparation needed to plan an appealing buffet.

   - Be sure each food item is easy to pick up.
   - Keep each food item to one or two bites.
   - Prepare flavorful items that go well with other foods being served but that do not dominate the taste buds.
   - Make items visually appealing.
   - Slice, shape, and portion mixed hors d'oeuvres carefully.
   - Include the proper sauces and utensils on the buffet tables.
   - Consider the overall color, shape, and look of the platter.
   - Be sure the cold food platter complements the overall buffet display.
   - Use attractive, durable platters that are suitable for what you're serving.

2. Using colored pencils or markers, draw the arrangement of each cold food platter on the platter drawings on the next page. Label each item of each platter. Identify the centerpiece and garnish of each cold food platter.

3. Diagram the buffet table layout. On a separate sheet of paper, draw the position of each cold food platter on the buffet tables. Indicate the service tool needed for each platter. Show the placement of the needed plates, napkins, toothpicks, and flatware. Label each item.

4. Share your project with the class. Display your cold food platter presentations and buffet table layouts to the class.

(Continued on next page)

Sandwich Production

Directions: In four teams, your class will be preparing hot, cold, grilled, and pizza sandwiches for lunch in your restaurant.

- **Team A:** Hot Sandwich
- **Team B:** Cold Sandwich
- **Team C:** Grilled Sandwich
- **Team D:** Pizza Sandwich

Each team will plan and prepare 10 sandwiches of their assigned type. Complete the steps that follow.

1. **Choose a recipe to prepare your team's type of sandwich.**
2. **Determine the ingredients to prepare 10 sandwiches.** Answer the following questions, and record your responses in the Sandwich Production chart on page 122:
   a. What type of bread will you use?
   b. What type of filling will you use?
   c. What type of spread will you use?
   d. What type of cheese will you use, if any?
3. **Determine the garnishes.** Record your selections in the Sandwich Production chart on page 122.
4. **Determine the sandwich cuts.** See the diagram on page 122. Circle the cut you want to use.
5. **Select your accompaniments.** Review the list below, and record your selections in the Sandwich Production chart:
   - Whole radishes, green onions, baby carrots, or cherry tomatoes
   - Carrot, celery, or summer squash sticks
   - Lettuce leaves or baby spinach leaves
   - Sliced cucumbers or tomatoes
   - Grilled, marinated vegetables
   - Pickle spears
   - Green or black olives
   - Slices of fruit
6. **Select the equipment needed for production.** List your selections in the Sandwich Production chart.
7. **Draw a diagram of your workspace.** On a separate sheet of paper, show the arrangement of the ingredients and utensils for sandwich making. Attach it to this activity sheet.
8. **Develop written production guidelines.** Write your guidelines on the Job Plan Sheet on page 123, detailing each step of the sandwich-making process.
9. **Make the sandwiches.** Set up your workspace according to your diagram. Then follow your production guidelines to test your workspace and method by making several sandwiches. Make any changes to the workspace or guidelines that improve efficiency.
10. **Rotate to another team's workspace.** Team A will rotate to Team B's workspace, Team B will rotate to Team C's workspace, Team C will rotate to Team D's workspace, and Team D will rotate to Team A's workspace. Make several sandwiches using the other team's workspace and following their production guidelines. Evaluate the other team's sandwich-making method.
11. **Compare your workspace and production guidelines with those of the other team.**

(Continued on next page)

Sandwich Production

Category	Selections
Sandwich type	
Bread	
Spread	
Filling	
Cheese	
Garnish	
Accompaniment(s)	
Utensils	

A.

B.

C.

(Continued on next page)

Name _____ Date _____

Job Plan Sheet

Recipe: _____

Yield: _____ **Portion size:** _____

Ingredient:	Amount:	Ingredient:	Amount:
_____	_____	_____	_____
_____	_____	_____	_____
_____	_____	_____	_____
_____	_____	_____	_____
_____	_____		

Equipment:	Use:	Equipment:	Use:
_____	_____	_____	_____
_____	_____	_____	_____
_____	_____	_____	_____

List each step in the preparation process below.

_____

_____

_____

_____

_____

_____

_____

_____

_____

_____

_____

_____

(Continued on next page)

Performance ✔ Checklist

Performance Standards
Level 4—Performs skill without supervision and adapts to problem situations.
Level 3—Performs skill satisfactorily without assistance or supervision.
Level 2—Performs skill satisfactorily, but requires assistance or supervision.
Level 1—Performs parts of skill satisfactorily, but requires considerable assistance or supervision.
Level 0—Cannot perform skill.

Attempt (circle one): 1   2   3   4

Comments: _____

_____

_____

_____

_____

Performance Level Achieved: _____

_____ 1. Demonstrates safety and sanitation practices while handling ingredients.

_____ 2. Plans job completely and professionally.

_____ 3. Uses firm, but tender bread.

_____ 4. Slices meats to the appropriate thickness.

_____ 5. Uses the correct amount of filling.

_____ 6. Uses the appropriate bread size for the amount of filling.

_____ 7. Cuts sandwiches cleanly and attractively, with nice height.

_____ 8. Garnishes the sandwich attractively and the toothpick is inserted correctly.

_____ 9. Uses sauces or condiments that are pleasing and do not overpower the sandwich.

_____ 10. Follows HACCP procedures at all times.

_____ 11. Prepares sandwiches to proper flavor, texture, temperature, and appearance.

Instructor's Signature: _____ **Date:** _____

Making Hot, Open-Face Sandwiches

Directions: Working in teams, plan and prepare to make 25 or less hot, open-face sandwiches to sell for lunch at your restaurant. Select the appropriate garnish and accompaniment for your sandwiches.

1. Choose a recipe for a hot, open-face sandwich, such as for a hot turkey or hot beef sandwich served with mashed potatoes and gravy.
2. Develop production guidelines and a workspace diagram on a separate sheet of paper. Your production guidelines should provide step-by-step sandwich-making procedures. Your workspace diagram should show the arrangement of all equipment, utensils, and ingredients. Be sure the ingredients and equipment are available in your lab.
3. Plan a garnish and accompaniment for your hot, open-face sandwiches.
4. Prepare and cook your sandwiches. Garnish and plate them. Serve the plate to another team.
5. Evaluate another team's plate.
6. Have your instructor complete the Performance Checklist below.

Performance ✔ Checklist

Performance Standards	**Attempt (circle one): 1 2 3 4**
Level 4—Performs skill without supervision and adapts to problem situations.	Comments: _____
Level 3—Performs skill satisfactorily without assistance or supervision.	_____
Level 2—Performs skill satisfactorily, but requires assistance or supervision.	_____
Level 1—Performs parts of skill satisfactorily, but requires considerable assistance or supervision.	_____
Level 0—Cannot perform skill.	**Performance Level Achieved:** _____

_____ 1. Demonstrates safety and sanitation practices at all times while handling ingredients.

_____ 2. Plans the job professionally and completely.

_____ 3. Uses firm, but tender bread.

_____ 4. Slices meats to the appropriate thickness.

_____ 5. The sandwich was garnished attractively; sauces or condiments were pleasing and did not overpower the sandwich.

_____ 6. Prepares sandwiches to proper flavor, texture, temperature, and appearance.

Instructor's Signature: _____   **Date:** _____

Name _____ Date _____

Grilled Ham & Cheese Production

Directions: Working in teams, prepare grilled ham and cheese sandwich by following the recipe below.

Grilled Ham and Cheese Sandwich

COOKING TECHNIQUE:
Grill

Grill/Broil:
1. Clean and heat the grill/broiler.
2. To prevent sticking, brush the food product with oil.

HACCP:
Hold at 140° or above.

HAZARDOUS FOODS:
Ham
Cheese

NUTRITION:
Calories: 440
Fat: 28.1 g
Protein: 16.7 g

CHEF NOTE:
Do not prepare the sandwiches too far in advance, because they will become soggy.

YIELD: 50 SERVINGS   SERVING SIZE: 1 SANDWICH

INGREDIENTS:

5 loaves	Sliced sandwich bread
4 lbs.	Ham, boneless, cooked, cut into 1-ounce slices
3 lbs.	American cheese, sliced
1½ lbs.	Clarified butter

METHOD OF PREPARATION:

1. Lay out the bread slices on a clean, dry table.
2. Place one slice of ham and cheese on each second slice of bread.
3. Cover with the first slice of bread, and cut on an angle to create two triangle sandwiches.
4. Lightly coat with clarified butter.
5. Grill until golden brown on both sides.
6. Serve hot.

Performance ✔ Checklist

Performance Standards

Level 4—Performs skill without supervision and adapts to problem situations.

Level 3—Performs skill satisfactorily without assistance or supervision.

Level 2—Performs skill satisfactorily, but requires assistance or supervision.

Level 1—Performs parts of skill satisfactorily, but requires considerable assistance or supervision.

Level 0—Cannot perform skill.

Attempt (circle one):   1   2   3   4

Comments: _____
_____
_____
_____
_____

Performance Level Achieved: _____

_____ 1. Performs mise en place effectively for sandwich preparation.

_____ 2. Prepares sandwiches to proper flavor, texture, doneness, and appearance within the specified time.

Instructor's Signature: _____ **Date:** _____

Preparing Stock

Directions: Working in teams, prepare different stocks as directed in the steps that follow.

1. Write the procedure for making white stock and brown stock on a separate sheet of paper and attach it to this activity sheet.

2. Following the stock preparation procedures, prepare from scratch a quart of white stock (chicken) and a quart of brown stock (beef).

3. Select a cooling method from your text. List the steps for cooling the stocks below. Then cool the stocks following this procedure and HACCP guidelines. Set the stocks aside.

Cooling Procedure:

_____

_____

_____

_____

_____

_____

_____

_____

_____

_____

4. Gather the following food items:
   - Canned chicken bouillon or consommé
   - Granular chicken bouillon
   - Chicken bouillon cubes
   - Condensed prepared chicken base
   - Canned beef bouillon or consommé
   - Granular beef bouillon
   - Beef bouillon cubes
   - Condensed prepared beef base

5. Using eight separate sauce pans, prepare each food item according to package directions.

6. Reheat the white stock and brown stock following HACCP guidelines.

7. Taste test all of the stocks and record your findings in the charts that follow. Then rate each stock using the following scale:
   1=Poor; **2**=Fair; **3**=Good; **4**=Great.

(Continued on next page)

Chicken-Based Stocks

Product	Color and Clarity	Quality	Rating
Scratch stock (chicken)			
Canned chicken bouillon or consommé			
Granular chicken bouillon			
Chicken bouillon cubes			
Condensed prepared chicken base			

Beef-Based Stocks

Product	Color and Clarity	Quality	Rating
Scratch stock (beef)			
Canned beef bouillon or consommé			
Granular beef bouillon			
Beef bouillon cubes			
Condensed prepared beef base			

(Continued on next page)

8. Present your white stock and brown stock to your instructor for evaluation, and have the Performance Checklist below completed.

Performance ✔ Checklist

Performance Standards	**Attempt (circle one): 1 2 3 4**
Level 4—Performs skill without supervision and adapts to problem situations.	Comments: _____
Level 3—Performs skill satisfactorily without assistance or supervision.	_____
Level 2—Performs skill satisfactorily, but requires assistance or supervision.	_____
Level 1—Performs parts of skill satisfactorily, but requires considerable assistance or supervision.	_____
Level 0—Cannot perform skill.	**Performance Level Achieved:** _____

_____ 1. Performs mise en place correctly. Team members are prepared.

_____ 2. Plans job fully and professionally.

_____ 3. Cools stock from 140°F to below 41°F following HACCP procedures.

_____ 4. Stocks maintain good color and clarity.

_____ 5. Stocks are reheated to 165°F, following HACCP procedures.

_____ 6. Follows safety and sanitation procedures at all times.

Instructor's Signature: _____ **Date:** _____

Creating a Mother Sauce

Directions: Divide into five teams, teams A–E. Working in teams, prepare a mother sauce. Follow the steps below.

1. Prepare your assigned mother sauce as follows:

   Team A: Espagnole   **Team D:** Velouté

   Team B: Tomato   **Team E:** Hollandaise

   Team C: Béchamel

2. All teams evaluate the others' mother sauces for quality and flavor. Rate each using the following scale:

   1=Poor; **2**=Fair; **3**=Good; **4**=Great.

3. Have your instructor evaluate your mother sauce using the Performance Checklist that follows.

4. **Optional rotation.** After preparing the team's assigned mother sauce, teams can rotate until each team prepares each mother sauce. Use each other's work plans for preparing mother sauces.

Performance ✔ Checklist

Performance Standards

Level 4—Performs skill without supervision and adapts to problem situations.

Level 3—Performs skill satisfactorily without assistance or supervision.

Level 2—Performs skill satisfactorily, but requires assistance or supervision.

Level 1—Performs parts of skill satisfactorily, but requires considerable assistance or supervision.

Level 0—Cannot perform skill.

Attempt (circle one):   1   2   3   4

Comments: _____

_____

_____

_____

_____

_____

Performance Level Achieved: _____

_____ 1. Performs mise en place correctly. Team members are prepared.

_____ 2. Plans job fully and professionally.

_____ 3. Thickens and simmers sauces properly.

_____ 4. Follows safety and sanitation procedures at all times.

_____ 5. Prepares sauce to proper flavor, consistency, doneness, and appearance.

Instructor's Signature: _____   **Date:** _____

Preparing Béchamel Sauce

Directions: Working in teams, prepare Béchamel sauce using the recipe that follows. Rate the sauce for proper flavor, consistency and appearance. Use the following scale: **1**=Poor; **2**=Fair; **3**=Good; **4**=Great.

COOKING TECHNIQUE:
Simmer

Simmer:
1. Heat the cooking liquid to the proper temperature.
2. Submerge the food product completely.
3. Keep the cooked product moist and warm.

GLOSSARY:
Clouté: studded with cloves
Chinois: cone-shaped strainer
Bain-marie: hot-water bath

HACCP:

Hold at 140°F or above, or cool to an internal temperature of 41°F or below.

HAZARDOUS FOOD:
Milk

NUTRITION:
Calories: 67.2
Fat: 4.23 g
Protein: 2.34 g

CHEF NOTES:
1. Béchamel sauce is a basic white cream sauce consisting simply of thickened, seasoned milk. Béchamel is often used as a binding agent or to make compound sauces.
2. The sauce is ready when the proper thickness has been achieved and the "floury" taste is cooked away.
3. To prevent a dried surface (skin) from forming while holding the sauce in a **bain-marie**, cover the surface with plastic wrap.

Béchamel Sauce

YIELD: 1 GAL.   SERVING SIZE: 2 OZ.

INGREDIENTS:

4 qts.	Milk
1 each	Onion **clouté**, cut in half
6 oz.	Clarified butter
6 oz.	All-purpose flour, sifted
	Salt and ground white pepper, to taste
	Nutmeg, to taste

METHOD OF PREPARATION:

1. In a saucepan, heat the milk with the onion **clouté**, and simmer for 10 minutes.

2. In another saucepan, heat the clarified butter over moderate heat.

3. Gradually add flour to make a blonde roux. Using a spoon, mix the roux thoroughly, and cook it approximately 5–6 minutes. Remove from the heat, and cool slightly.

4. Remove the onion clouté from the milk.

5. Gradually add the hot milk to the roux, whisking constantly. Heat to a boil; reduce to a simmer. Simmer for 20 minutes or until the proper flavor and consistency are achieved.

6. Season to taste.

7. Strain through a fine **chinois** into a suitable container. Hold at 140°F or above, or cool to an internal temperature of 41°F or below. Label, date, and refrigerate.

8. Reheat to 165°F for 15 seconds.

Preparing Beef Consommé

Directions: Working in teams, prepare beef consommé using the recipe that follows. Rate the consommé for proper flavor, consistency, and appearance: **1**=Poor; **2**=Fair; **3**=Good; **4**=Great.

COOKING TECHNIQUES:
Simmer, Boil

Simmer & Poach:
1. Heat the cooking liquid to the proper temperature.
2. Submerge the food product completely.
3. Keep the cooked product moist and warm.

Boil: (at sea level)
1. Bring the cooking liquid to a rapid boil.
2. Stir the contents, and cook the food product throughout.
3. Serve hot.

GLOSSARY:
Mirepoix: roughly chopped vegetables
Brunoise: ⅛-in. dice
Marmite: stockpot
Chinois: fine, cone-shaped strainer

HACCP:
Hold at 140°F or above.
Cool to 41°F or below.

HAZARDOUS FOODS:
Egg whites
Ground beef

NUTRITION:
Calories: 116
Fat: 4.34 g
Protein: 13.8 g

Beef Consommé

YIELD: 50 SERVINGS   SERVING SIZE: 8 OZ.

INGREDIENTS:

5 gal.	Cold brown beef stock or strong beef broth
10 each	Egg whites, slightly whipped
3 lbs.	Ground beef, lean
16 each	Black peppercorns
6 each	Bay leaves
3 oz.	Parsley stems
1½ tsp.	Thyme leaves

MIREPOIX:

12 oz.	Onion, peeled, cut **brunoise**
2 lbs.	Carrots, washed, peeled, cut brunoise
4 stalks	Celery, washed, trimmed, cut brunoise
2 pts.	Tomato purée

METHOD OF PREPARATION:

1. In a mixing bowl, combine the lean ground beef, **mirepoix**, tomato purée, herbs, spices, salt, and white pepper to taste. Mix the egg whites and meat mixture until blended. Refrigerate.
2. In a **marmite**, blend the cold beef stock with the above clarifying ingredients.
3. Place on moderate heat. Carefully watch the clarifying ingredients to make sure they do not scorch. Stir occasionally, until a raft forms. Then stop stirring.
4. Simmer the soup for 1½ hours or to the desired strength, making sure the raft does not break or sink. Remove the first cup of consommé through the spigot, and discard.
5. In a **chinois** lined with four to five layers of wet cheesecloth, slowly strain the liquid into a soup insert, separating the clarifying ingredients from the liquid. Hold at 140°F or above.
6. Adjust the seasonings. Remove all of the fat from the consommé, and serve very hot with the appropriate garnish.
7. Cool to an internal temperature of 41°F or below.
8. Reheat to 165°F for 15 seconds.

Soup Production

Directions: Working in teams, prepare and garnish a soup. Complete the steps that follow.

Part A

1. Select one of the following types of soups to prepare: consommé, vegetable, puree, cream, bisque, cooked cold, uncooked cold, chowder, or international. Choose an approved recipe.

2. Review the recipe. Convert the yield to make 2 quarts of soup. Use this conversion formula:

   Step 1 desired yield ÷ existing yield = conversion factor

   Step 2 existing quantity × conversion factor = desired quantity

3. Gather all equipment, utensils, and ingredients. Follow the converted recipe to prepare two quarts of soup.

4. Select and use an appropriate garnish. The type of garnish will depend on the soup.

5. Complete the Soup Production worksheet below.

6. Have your instructor sample your soup and complete the Performance Checklist on page 134.

Part B

1. Cool your leftover soup using an approved method.

2. Store the soup properly.

3. Have your instructor inspect your soup and complete the Performance Checklist on page 134.

Soup Production

Name and type of soup: _____

Thickening agent or method: _____

Production procedures: _____

_____

_____

_____

_____

_____

Serving temperature: _____

(Continued on next page)

Performance ✔ Checklist

Performance Standards

Level 4—Performs skill without supervision and adapts to problem situations.

Level 3—Performs skill satisfactorily without assistance or supervision.

Level 2—Performs skill satisfactorily, but requires assistance or supervision.

Level 1—Performs parts of skill satisfactorily, but requires considerable assistance or supervision.

Level 0—Cannot perform skill.

Attempt (circle one): 1 2 3 4

Comments: _____

_____

_____

_____

_____

_____

Performance Level Achieved: _____

_____ 1. Performs mise en place correctly. Team members are prepared.

_____ 2. Accurately adjusts the recipe to make two quarts.

_____ 3. Observes the correct proportion of liquid to ingredients.

_____ 4. The soup possesses good consistency.

_____ 5. The ingredients are tender and hold their shape.

_____ 6. The soup is not cloudy, pasty, off flavor, salty, fatty, overcooked, or watery.

_____ 7. The soup is garnished attractively and is served neatly in the bowl.

_____ 8. The soup is flavorful and served at the proper temperature.

_____ 9. The soup is cooled correctly, following any safety and sanitation procedures.

_____ 10. The soup is stored correctly, following any safety and sanitation procedures.

Instructor's Signature: _____ **Date:** _____

Hot Appetizer Production

Directions: Working in teams, prepare a plated hot appetizer. Then, using each team's hot appetizer recipe, plan a hot appetizer buffet for 50 people.

Part A

1. Select one of the following hot appetizer categories:
   - Brochettes
   - Filled pastry shells
   - Meatballs
   - Rumaki
   - Stuffed potato skins
   - Chicken wings
2. Choose a recipe within your category that is made with affordable ingredients. Submit the recipe to your instructor for approval.
3. Use the formula that follows and convert the yield of the recipe to prepare four servings.
   Step 1 desired yield ÷ existing yield = conversion factor
   Step 2 existing quantity × conversion factor = desired quantity
4. Select an appropriate garnish.
5. Choose a plate or tray that has an interesting shape or size. On a separate sheet of paper, draw the arrangement of the hot appetizer on the plate or tray with the selected garnish. Label the parts.
6. Gather all equipment, utensils, and ingredients. Prepare the converted recipe.
7. Present your team's appetizers and production procedures to the class.
8. Have your instructor complete the Performance Checklist on page 136.

Part B

1. Collect a copy of all the recipes from Part A. Use them to plan a buffet for 50 people.
2. Convert the yield of each recipe to serve 50 people.
3. Draw the plate setup for each of the appetizers on the diagrams that follow. Label all parts.
4. On a separate sheet of paper, draw the table arrangement. Label all parts.

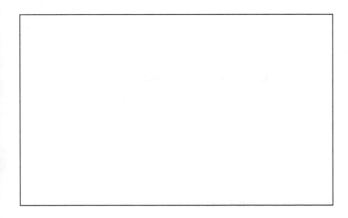 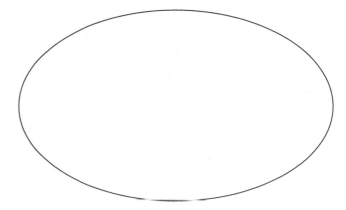

(Continued on next page)

Performance ✔ Checklist

Performance Standards

Level 4—Performs skill without supervision and adapts to problem situations.

Level 3—Performs skill satisfactorily without assistance or supervision.

Level 2—Performs skill satisfactorily, but requires assistance or supervision.

Level 1—Performs parts of skill satisfactorily, but requires considerable assistance or supervision.

Level 0—Cannot perform skill.

Attempt (circle one): 1   2   3   4

Comments: _____

_____

_____

_____

_____

_____

Performance Level Achieved: _____

_____ 1. Performs mise en place correctly. Team members are prepared.

_____ 2. Accurately converts the recipe to serve 50 people.

_____ 3. Outlines production procedures correctly.

_____ 4. Prepares hot appetizers to proper flavor, temperature, and appearance.

Instructor's Signature: _____ **Date:** _____

Cutting & Cooking Fish

Directions: In teams, demonstrate how to cut and cook different market forms of fish by completing the steps below.

1. Practice cutting drawn or dressed fish into fillets, steaks, and butterflied portions.
2. Choose a cooking method, recipe, and garnish for your fish.
3. Complete the Job Plan Sheet on page 138. Submit it to your instructor for approval.
4. Cook your fish following your recipe and approved Job Plan Sheet.
5. Plate, garnish, and serve your fish to another team and your instructor.
6. Have your instructor complete the Performance Checklist below.

Performance ✔ Checklist

Performance Standards

Level 4—Performs skill without supervision and adapts to problem situations.

Level 3—Performs skill satisfactorily without assistance or supervision.

Level 2—Performs skill satisfactorily, but requires assistance or supervision.

Level 1—Performs parts of skill satisfactorily, but requires considerable assistance or supervision.

Level 0—Cannot perform skill.

Attempt (circle one):   1   2   3   4

Comments: _____

_____

_____

_____

_____

_____

Performance Level Achieved: _____

_____ 1. Cuts fish into fillets.

_____ 2. Cuts fish into steaks.

_____ 3. Cuts fish into butterflied portions.

_____ 4. Follows knife safety rules at all times.

_____ 5. Cooks fish to 145°F for 15 seconds.

_____ 6. Prepares fish to proper flavor and appearance.

_____ 7. Plates, garnishes, and serves fish appropriately.

_____ 8. Stores fish safely and according to HACCP procedures.

Instructor's Signature: _____   **Date:** _____

(Continued on next page)

Job Plan Sheet

Recipe: _____

Yield: _____   Portion size: _____

Ingredient:	Amount:	Ingredient:	Amount:
_____	_____	_____	_____
_____	_____	_____	_____
_____	_____	_____	_____
_____	_____	_____	_____
_____	_____	_____	_____

Equipment:	Use:	Equipment:	Use:
_____	_____	_____	_____
_____	_____	_____	_____
_____	_____	_____	_____

List each preparation step below.

_____

_____

_____

_____

_____

_____

_____

_____

_____

_____

_____

_____

Selecting Fish & Shellfish

Directions: Complete the steps that follow to determine how to select fish and shellfish.

Part A

Price by unit each piece of fish and shellfish in the chart below. Then answer the questions that follow.

Fish or Shellfish	Unit	Cost per Unit
Trout		
Shrimp (Jumbo)		
Cod		
Crab legs (Alaskan King)		
Maine lobster		
Salmon		

1. Which piece of fish or shellfish is the most expensive by unit?

   _____

   _____

2. Which piece of fish or shellfish is the most economical?

   _____

   _____

3. Which items would you most likely find on a family-style menu? Explain why.

   _____

   _____

   _____

   _____

   _____

(Continued on next page)

Part B

Read each situation in the chart below. Determine whether you should select the piece of fish or shell-fish described. Then explain why or why not in the chart.

Situation	Your Response
The whole fish are slimy.	
The crabs are warm and have a strange odor.	
The meat of the flounder does not separate when the fillet is bent.	
The raw shrimp in the shell is brown in color.	
The clams are sandy on the inside.	
The ocean bass smells like seaweed.	
The gills on the flounder are pink.	
The eyes of the catfish are sunken.	
Ice is inside the frozen trout.	
The lobsters are alive and brown in color.	

Culinary Essentials Lab Manual
Copyright © Glencoe/McGraw-Hill

Cooking Fish or Shellfish

Directions: Work in teams to cook and garnish fish or shellfish in a variety of ways. Complete the steps that follow.

1. **Select a fish or shellfish to cook.**
2. **Choose a cooking technique.**
3. **Select a recipe.** Choose an appropriate recipe for the seafood selected.
4. **Complete the Job Plan Sheet on page 142.** Gather all equipment, utensils, and ingredients. Select seasonings and the garnish. Submit your recipe and Job Plan Sheet for approval.
5. **Prepare your seafood dish.** Follow your approved Job Plan Sheet.
6. **Plate and garnish your seafood dish.** Have your instructor evaluate your work and complete the Performance Checklist below.

Performance ✔ Checklist

Performance Standards

Level 4—Performs skill without supervision and adapts to problem situations.

Level 3—Performs skill satisfactorily without assistance or supervision.

Level 2—Performs skill satisfactorily, but requires assistance or supervision.

Level 1—Performs parts of skill satisfactorily, but requires considerable assistance or supervision.

Level 0—Cannot perform skill.

Attempt (circle one):   1   2   3   4

Comments: _____

_____

_____

_____

_____

_____

Performance Level Achieved: _____

_____ 1. Performs mise en place correctly. Team members are prepared.

_____ 2. Plans job fully and professionally.

_____ 3. Selects and uses an appropriate garnish.

_____ 4. Seafood market form is easy to recognize.

_____ 5. Seafood is the appropriate color with opaque flesh.

_____ 6. Seafood is tender and flaky.

_____ 7. Broiled, grilled, sautéed, or pan-fried fish is slightly browned and crispy with juicy and tender interior.

_____ 8. Deep-fried fish with batter is rich golden brown with juicy and tender interior.

_____ 9. Seafood is cooked to an internal temperature of 145°F for 15 seconds.

_____ 10. Seafood is neat and attractively plated.

_____ 11. Follows safety and sanitation procedures at all times.

Instructor's Signature: _____ **Date:** _____

(Continued on next page)

Job Plan Sheet

Recipe: _____

Yield: _____ Portion size: _____

Ingredient:	Amount:	Ingredient:	Amount:
_____	_____	_____	_____
_____	_____	_____	_____
_____	_____	_____	_____
_____	_____	_____	_____
_____	_____	_____	_____

Equipment:	Use:	Equipment:	Use:
_____	_____	_____	_____
_____	_____	_____	_____
_____	_____	_____	_____

List each preparation step below.

_____

_____

_____

_____

_____

_____

_____

_____

_____

_____

_____

_____

Fish & Shellfish Math

Directions: Complete the following math problems. Show your calculations in the space provided.

1. A seafood vendor offers you a 20% discount off the total price if you purchase 25 gallons of oysters. Each gallon sells for $70.00. If you bought 25 gallons of oysters, what would be your price without the discount? What would be your price *with* the discount?

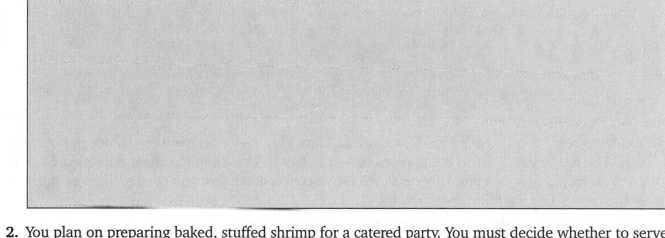

2. You plan on preparing baked, stuffed shrimp for a catered party. You must decide whether to serve 5 shrimp per person at 15 count per pound, or 4 shrimp per person at 12 count per pound. The shrimp at 15 count per pound cost $11.95 per pound? The shrimp at 12 count per pound cost $13.95 per pound. Which shrimp purchase is the best value?

(Continued on next page)

3. A fish vendor offers salmon in two forms: drawn fish or skin-on fillets. The drawn fish sells for $3.95 per pound. After filleting a 9-lb. fish, you determine that your trim loss is 35% per pound. The fillets sell for $5.25 per pound with only 5% trim loss per pound. Which form of salmon is the best value?

4. You have been given a recipe for New England Clam Chowder to prepare for an upcoming reception. The recipe yields 20 10-oz. portions served in bowls. The reception client requested 50 6-oz. portions served in soup cups. Determine the recipe conversion factor you need to increase the yield of the recipe. Use the following formulas:

existing portions × existing portion size = total existing yield

desired portions × desired portion size = new yield

existing yield ÷ new yield = conversion factor

Cutting Poultry

Directions: Work in teams. Complete the steps below.

1. Inspect the bird provided by your instructor.
2. Record the type of poultry and its classification and age. Describe the quality characteristics of your bird in the space that follows.

_____

_____

_____

_____

_____

3. Cut the poultry provided to your team into pieces as shown in your text.
4. Have your instructor check your work and complete the Performance Checklist below.

Performance ✔ Checklist

Performance Standards	
Level 4—Performs skill without supervision and adapts to problem situations.	**Attempt (circle one): 1 2 3 4**
	Comments: _____
Level 3—Performs skill satisfactorily without assistance or supervision.	_____
	_____
Level 2—Performs skill satisfactorily, but requires assistance or supervision.	_____
	_____
Level 1—Performs parts of skill satisfactorily, but requires considerable assistance or supervision.	_____
Level 0—Cannot perform skill.	**Performance Level Achieved:** _____

_____ 1. Evaluates poultry accurately according to quality characteristics identified in the text.

_____ 2. Cuts poultry up correctly.

_____ 3. Follows safety and sanitation procedures at all times.

_____ 4. Follows HACCP procedures at all times.

Instructor's Signature: _____   **Date:** _____

Cooking Poultry with Moist Heat

Directions: Work in teams. Complete the steps for cooking poultry with moist heat below.

1. Select a recipe for poaching or simmering poultry that includes a sauce.

2. Prepare the poultry for poaching or simmering as directed in your recipe.

3. Bring the cooking liquid to just below the boiling point. Poaching temperatures range from 150°F to 185°F. Simmering temperatures range from 185°F to 200°F.

4. Place the poultry in the liquid and cook at a constant temperature until done. Cook to an internal temperature of 165°F for 15 seconds.

5. Remove the cooked poultry from the cooking liquid and prepare the sauce as directed in your recipe.

6. Taste your poultry for proper flavor, texture, and temperature.

7. Have your instructor evaluate your poultry using the Performance Checklist below.

Performance ✔ Checklist

Performance Standards
Level 4—Performs skill without supervision and adapts to problem situations.
Level 3—Performs skill satisfactorily without assistance or supervision.
Level 2—Performs skill satisfactorily, but requires assistance or supervision.
Level 1—Performs parts of skill satisfactorily, but requires considerable assistance or supervision.
Level 0—Cannot perform skill.

Attempt (circle one):   1   2   3   4

Comments: _____

_____

_____

_____

_____

_____

Performance Level Achieved: _____

_____ 1. Performs mise en place correctly.

_____ 2. Follows safety and sanitation procedures at all times.

_____ 3. Prepares poultry to proper flavor, texture, doneness, and appearance.

Instructor's Signature: _____ **Date:** _____

Cooking Poultry with Dry Heat

Directions: Work in teams to cook and garnish poultry. Complete the steps that follow.

1. **Select a type of poultry to cook.**
2. **Choose a dry heat cooking technique.**
3. **Select a recipe with 8 ingredients or less.**
4. **Complete the Job Plan Sheet on page 148.** Make a list of all the necessary ingredients. Select the seasonings and the garnish. Submit your recipe and Job Plan Sheet for approval.
5. **Perform mise en place.** Gather all the equipment, utensils, and ingredients.
6. **Prepare your poultry dish.** Follow your Job Plan Sheet.
7. **Plate and garnish your poultry dish.** Have your instructor evaluate your work and complete the Performance Checklist below.

Performance ✔ Checklist

Performance Standards	Attempt (circle one): 1 2 3 4
Level 4—Performs skill without supervision and adapts to problem situations.	Comments: _____
Level 3—Performs skill satisfactorily without assistance or supervision.	_____
Level 2—Performs skill satisfactorily, but requires assistance or supervision.	_____
Level 1—Performs parts of skill satisfactorily, but requires considerable assistance or supervision.	_____
Level 0—Cannot perform skill.	Performance Level Achieved: _____

_____ 1. Performs mise en place correctly.

_____ 2. Plans job fully and professionally.

_____ 3. Follows safety and sanitation procedures at all times.

_____ 4. Prepares poultry to proper flavor, texture, doneness, and appearance.

_____ 5. Presents poultry neatly and attractively.

_____ 6. Selects and uses an appropriate garnish.

Instructor's Signature: _____   **Date:** _____

(Continued on next page)

Job Plan Sheet

Recipe: _____

Yield: _____   Portion size: _____

Ingredient:	Amount:	Ingredient:	Amount:
_____	_____	_____	_____
_____	_____	_____	_____
_____	_____	_____	_____
_____	_____	_____	_____
_____	_____	_____	_____

Equipment:	Use:	Equipment:	Use:
_____	_____	_____	_____
_____	_____	_____	_____
_____	_____	_____	_____

List each preparation step below.

_____

_____

_____

_____

_____

_____

_____

_____

_____

_____

_____

_____

Identifying Cuts of Meat

Directions, Part A: Review the beef bone shapes and primal cuts of meat in the chart below. Name one fabricated cut for each primal cut listed below.

Bone	Major Bone	Primal Cut	Fabricated Cut
	Arm bone	Chuck	
	Leg or Round bone	Round	
	Back bone or T-bone	Loin	
	Wedge bone	Loin, near round	
	Flat bone	Loin, center cuts	
	Pin bone	Loin	
	Blade bone (neck area)	Chuck	
	Blade bone (center cut)	Rib	
	Blade bone (rib area)	Rib	
	Back and rib bone	Rib Loin	
	Breast and rib bones	Brisket Plate Flank	

(Continued on next page)

Directions, Part B: Divide into four teams. Identify fabricated cuts of meat by completing the steps that follow.

1. On a piece of poster board, draw an outline carcass of your team's assigned type of meat, such as beef, pork, lamb, or veal. Divide the outline into the primal cuts according to the illustrations in your textbook.

2. Draw and cut out each of the fabricated cuts on a different color of paper. Attach each fabricated cut to its appropriate primal cut on the poster.

3. Label each primal cut with the bone shapes characteristic of that cut.

4. Label which cuts are tender and which cuts are less tender.

5. Complete the chart above. Write in the fabricated cuts of each primal cut.

6. Share your poster and chart with the rest of the class. Discuss how the primal cuts are similar to each other in muscle and bone shape. Display the posters in your commercial kitchen laboratory.

7. Have your instructor complete the Performance Checklist below.

Performance ✔ Checklist

Performance Standards	Attempt (circle one): 1 2 3 4
Level 4—Performs skill without supervision and adapts to problem situations.	Comments: _____
Level 3—Performs skill satisfactorily without assistance or supervision.	_____
Level 2—Performs skill satisfactorily, but requires assistance or supervision.	_____
Level 1—Performs parts of skill satisfactorily, but requires considerable assistance or supervision.	_____
Level 0—Cannot perform skill.	Performance Level Achieved: _____

_____ 1. Carcass outline correctly identifies each primal cut.

_____ 2. The corresponding fabricated cut is attached to the appropriate primal cut.

_____ 3. Bone shapes are correctly identified.

_____ 4. Degree of tenderness for each cut of meat is indicated.

_____ 5. The poster shows that the student has a strong understanding of primal cuts, fabricated cuts, and bone shapes.

Instructor's Signature: _____ Date: _____

Meat Preparation

Directions: Work in teams to cook a cut of meat. Complete the steps that follow.

1. **Select a cut of meat to cook.**
2. **Choose a cooking technique.**
3. **Select a recipe.**
4. **Complete the Job Plan Sheet on page 152.** Make a list of all necessary ingredients.
5. **Perform mise en place.** Gather all equipment, utensils, and ingredients. Then have your instructor approve your Job Plan Sheet before going on to the next step.
6. **Prepare your meat.** Follow your Job Plan Sheet.
7. **Present the dish to your instructor.** Have your instructor complete the Performance Checklist.

Performance ✔ Checklist

Performance Standards
Level 4—Performs skill without supervision and adapts to problem situations.
Level 3—Performs skill satisfactorily without assistance or supervision.
Level 2—Performs skill satisfactorily, but requires assistance or supervision.
Level 1—Performs parts of skill satisfactorily, but requires considerable assistance or supervision.
Level 0—Cannot perform skill.

Attempt (circle one):   1   2   3   4

Comments: _____

_____

_____

_____

_____

_____

Performance Level Achieved: _____

_____ 1. Demonstrates safety and sanitation practices while handling raw meat.

_____ 2. Performs mise en place correctly.

_____ 3. Plans job professionally and completely.

_____ 4. Cooking technique is executed appropriately.

_____ 5. Meat is cooked to a safe internal temperature for the type of meat.

_____ 6. Follows HACCP procedures at all times.

_____ 7. Prepares meat to proper flavor, texture, doneness, and appearance.

Instructor's Signature: _____ **Date:** _____

(Continued on next page)

Job Plan Sheet

Recipe: _____

Yield: _____   Portion size: _____

Ingredient:	Amount:	Ingredient:	Amount:
_____	_____	_____	_____
_____	_____	_____	_____
_____	_____	_____	_____
_____	_____	_____	_____
_____	_____	_____	_____

Equipment:	Use:	Equipment:	Use:
_____	_____	_____	_____
_____	_____	_____	_____
_____	_____	_____	_____

List each preparation step below.

_____

_____

_____

_____

_____

_____

_____

_____

_____

_____

_____

_____

Identifying Pasta

Directions: Complete the chart by following the steps below.

Part A

1. Describe the quality standards of each type of pasta.
2. Explain the best way to prepare and cook each type of pasta.

Type of Pasta	Quality Standards	Preparation & Cooking Method
Egg noodles		
Manicotti		
Orzo		
Linguine		
Conchiglie		
Farfalle		

(Continued on next page)

Part B

1. Select three types of pasta described in the chart on the preceding page. Write your selections in the spaces provided below.

2. For each pasta:
   - Describe a filling or sauce you might use with the pasta.
   - Explain how you might serve, or plate, the pasta—as part of a salad, as a main course, or as a substitute for potatoes or rice.
   - Describe how to store the pasta.

Type of pasta: _____

_____

_____

_____

_____

_____

Type of pasta: _____

_____

_____

_____

_____

_____

Type of pasta: _____

_____

_____

_____

_____

_____

Name _____ Date _____

Using Asian Noodles

Directions, Part A: Using print or Internet resources, research the following types of Asian noodles. Describe the characteristics of each noodle. Then, identify a dish and its country of origin for which each type of noodle could be used.

Noodle Type	Noodle Characteristics	Noodle Dish & Country of Origin
Clear Vermicelli		
Chinese Egg Noodles		
Egg Roll Skins		
Rice Noodles		
Rice Sticks		
Rice Papers		
Buckwheat Noodles		
Somen Noodles		
Cellophane Noodles		

(Continued on next page)

Directions, Part B: As a team, select a type of Asian noodle to prepare. Then complete the steps below.

1. Locate a recipe with which to use your chosen noodle.

   Name of recipe: _____

   Type of noodle used: _____

   Other recipe ingredients: _____

   _____

   _____

   _____

   _____

2. Prepare the recipe.
3. Rate your final product using the following scale: **1**=Poor, **2**=Fair, **3**=Good, **4**=Great.
4. Share your results with the class.
5. Have your instructor evaluate your Asian noodle dish using the Performance Checklist.

Performance ✔ Checklist

Performance Standards	**Attempt (circle one):** 1 2 3 4
Level 4—Performs skill without supervision and adapts to problem situations.	Comments: _____
Level 3—Performs skill satisfactorily without assistance or supervision.	
Level 2—Performs skill satisfactorily, but requires assistance or supervision.	
Level 1—Performs parts of skill satisfactorily, but requires considerable assistance or supervision.	
Level 0—Cannot perform skill.	**Performance Level Achieved:** _____

_____ 1. Demonstrates safety and sanitation during preparation and cooking.

_____ 2. Plans job professionally and completely.

_____ 3. Executes cooking technique appropriately.

_____ 4. Follows HACCP procedures at all times.

_____ 5. Prepares pasta to proper flavor, texture, doneness, and appearance.

Instructor's Signature: _____   **Date:** _____

Cooking Pasta

Directions: Working in teams, prepare a pasta entrée for a party of five. Control portion sizes. Complete the steps that follow.

1. **Select a pasta recipe.**
2. **Complete the Job Plan Sheet on page 158.** Submit it to your instructor for approval.
3. **Perform mise en place.** Gather the equipment, utensils, and ingredients. Follow the recipe and your approved Job Plan Sheet to prepare the pasta dish.
4. **Cook the pasta.** Plate and garnish the dish. Then, present it to your instructor for evaluation.

Performance ✔ Checklist

Performance Standards

Level 4—Performs skill without supervision and adapts to problem situations.

Level 3—Performs skill satisfactorily without assistance or supervision.

Level 2—Performs skill satisfactorily, but requires assistance or supervision.

Level 1—Performs parts of skill satisfactorily, but requires considerable assistance or supervision.

Level 0—Cannot perform skill.

Attempt (circle one):   1   2   3   4

Comments: _____

_____

_____

_____

_____

_____

Performance Level Achieved: _____

_____ 1. Demonstrates safety and sanitation during preparation and cooking.

_____ 2. Plans job professionally and completely.

_____ 3. Executes cooking technique appropriately.

_____ 4. Follows HACCP procedures at all times.

_____ 5. Prepares pasta to proper flavor, texture, doneness, and appearance.

Instructor's Signature: _____   **Date:** _____

(Continued on next page)

Job Plan Sheet

Recipe: _____

Yield: _____   Portion size: _____

Ingredient:	Amount:	Ingredient:	Amount:
_____	_____	_____	_____
_____	_____	_____	_____
_____	_____	_____	_____
_____	_____	_____	_____

Equipment:	Use:	Equipment:	Use:
_____	_____	_____	_____
_____	_____	_____	_____
_____	_____	_____	_____

List each preparation step below.

_____

_____

_____

_____

_____

_____

_____

_____

_____

_____

_____

_____

_____

Name _____ Date _____

Cooking Rice & Grains

Directions: Working in teams, plan and prepare one rice dish or one grain dish. Complete the steps that follow.

1. **Select a rice or a grain recipe to prepare.**
2. **Review the recipe.** Convert the amount of ingredients so that each rice or grain dish will serve four.
3. **Complete the Job Plan Sheet on page 160.** Submit it to your instructor for approval.
4. **Perform mise en place.** Gather the equipment, utensils, and ingredients you will need, including any seasonings or garnishes.
5. **Prepare and cook the rice or grain dish.** Follow your approved Job Plan Sheet.
6. **Present your completed dish to your instructor for evaluation.** Have your instructor complete the Performance Checklist below.

Performance ✔ Checklist

Performance Standards

Level 4—Performs skill without supervision and adapts to problem situations.

Level 3—Performs skill satisfactorily without assistance or supervision.

Level 2—Performs skill satisfactorily, but requires assistance or supervision.

Level 1—Performs parts of skill satisfactorily, but requires considerable assistance or supervision.

Level 0—Cannot perform skill.

Attempt (circle one):   1   2   3   4

Comments: _____

_____

_____

_____

_____

_____

Performance Level Achieved: _____

_____ 1. Demonstrates safety and sanitation practices during preparation and cooking.

_____ 2. Plans job professionally and completely.

_____ 3. Executes cooking technique appropriately.

_____ 4. Cooks rice or grain to the appropriate degree of doneness. Holds at 140°F or above if necessary.

_____ 5. Follows HACCP procedures at all times.

_____ 6. Prepares rice or grain to proper flavor, texture, tenderness, and appearance.

Instructor's Signature: _____ **Date:** _____

(Continued on next page)

Job Plan Sheet

Recipe: _____

Yield: _____   Portion size: _____

Ingredient:	Amount:	Ingredient:	Amount:
_____	_____	_____	_____
_____	_____	_____	_____
_____	_____	_____	_____
_____	_____	_____	_____
_____	_____	_____	_____

Equipment:	Use:	Equipment:	Use:
_____	_____	_____	_____
_____	_____	_____	_____
_____	_____	_____	_____

List each preparation step below.

_____

_____

_____

_____

_____

_____

_____

_____

_____

_____

_____

Name _____ Date _____

Ripening Fruit

Directions: Complete the steps that follow to ripen fruit.

1. Place one unripened apple, melon, or banana in a brown paper bag and seal it.
2. Observe the stages of ripening. Look for changes in color, firmness, and aroma. Check your fruit for changes after 24 hours. Record your results in the chart below.
3. Check your fruit again after 48 hours and again after 72 hours. Record your results in the chart.

Fruit	24 Hours	48 Hours	72 Hours

4. Answer the questions below.

A. What happens to fruit when it ripens?

_____

_____

B. Why will some fruits, such as apples, melons, and bananas, ripen in a sealed paper bag?

_____

_____

C. How can you prevent fruit from becoming overripe?

_____

_____

D. How can this process benefit food production in foodservice?

_____

_____

Preparing Fruit

Directions: Complete the steps that follow to zest, segment, and peel a piece of fruit.

1. Demonstrate how to zest, peel, and segment a piece of citrus fruit.
2. Practice each of the techniques. When you feel confident about your skill, have your instructor evaluate your work and complete the Performance Checklist below.

Performance ✔ Checklist

Performance Standards

Level 4—Performs skill without supervision and adapts to problem situations.

Level 3—Performs skill satisfactorily without assistance or supervision.

Level 2—Performs skill satisfactorily, but requires assistance or supervision.

Level 1—Performs parts of skill satisfactorily, but requires considerable assistance or supervision.

Level 0—Cannot perform skill.

Attempt (circle one):   1   2   3   4

Comments: _____

_____

_____

_____

_____

Performance Level Achieved: _____

_____ 1. Follows safety and sanitation practices at all times during this job, including washing the fruit prior to zesting, peeling, and segmenting.

_____ 2. Citrus fruit is zested properly.

_____ 3. Citrus fruit is peeled correctly.

_____ 4. Citrus fruit is segmented properly.

Instructor's Signature: _____   **Date:** _____

Cooking Fruit

Directions: Working in teams, practice cooking fruit using dry and moist cooking methods.

Dry Cooking

1. Select a dry cooking method for fruit: broiling, grilling, baking, sautéing, or deep-frying.
2. Find a fruit recipe that uses the cooking method you selected.
3. Prepare the Job Plan Sheet on page 164. Be sure all supplies are on hand before beginning.
4. Prepare and cook the fruit recipe, following your Job Plan Sheet.
5. Plate and garnish the finished product.
6. Have your instructor evaluate your finished product and complete the Performance Checklist.

Moist Cooking

1. Select a moist cooking method for fruit: poaching or simmering.
2. Find a fruit recipe that uses the cooking method you selected.
3. Prepare the Job Plan Sheet on page 164. Be sure all supplies are on hand before beginning.
4. Prepare and cook the fruit recipe, following your Job Plan Sheet.
5. Plate and garnish the finished product.
6. Have your instructor evaluate your finished product and complete the Performance Checklist.

Performance ✔ Checklist

Performance Standards

Level 4—Performs skill without supervision and adapts to problem situations.

Level 3—Performs skill satisfactorily without assistance or supervision.

Level 2—Performs skill satisfactorily, but requires assistance or supervision.

Level 1—Performs parts of skill satisfactorily, but requires considerable assistance or supervision.

Level 0—Cannot perform skill.

Attempt (circle one):   1   2   3   4

Comments: _____

_____

_____

_____

_____

_____

Performance Level Achieved: _____

_____ 1. Follows safety and sanitation practices at all times during this job.

_____ 2. Selects and executes cooking methods correctly.

_____ 3. Correctly prepares and follows the Job Plan Sheet during preparation and cooking.

_____ 4. The fruit is cooked to the appropriate degree of doneness.

_____ 5. The fruit retains its shape and has even, natural color.

_____ 6. The fruit's texture is moist, tender, and juicy.

_____ 7. The fruit has a delicate flavor and is aromatic.

_____ 8. The fruit is appropriately plated and artistically garnished.

Instructor's Signature: _____   **Date:** _____

(Continued on next page)

Job Plan Sheet

Recipe: _____

Yield: _____   Portion size: _____

Ingredient:	Amount:	Ingredient:	Amount:
_____	_____	_____	_____
_____	_____	_____	_____
_____	_____	_____	_____
_____	_____	_____	_____
_____	_____	_____	_____

Equipment:	Use:	Equipment:	Use:
_____	_____	_____	_____
_____	_____	_____	_____
_____	_____	_____	_____

List each preparation step below.

Dry cooking: _____   Moist cooking: _____

_____   _____

_____   _____

_____   _____

_____   _____

_____   _____

_____   _____

_____   _____

_____   _____

_____   _____

Potato Cookery

Directions: Working individually and in teams, complete the steps below.

Part A

1. Working individually, select a topic from the list below.
   - Mealy potatoes
   - Waxy potatoes
   - Russet potatoes
   - Red potatoes
   - Yukon potatoes
   - White sweet potatoes
   - Red sweet potatoes
   - Quality characteristics
   - Green potatoes
   - Fresh potatoes
   - Canned potatoes
   - Frozen potatoes
   - Dehydrated potatoes
   - Storage of potatoes

2. Research the information about your topic. Share your information with the class.

Part B

1. Working in teams, inspect the potatoes provided by your instructor. Identify each type of potato. Examine the skin color and texture. Then, cut each potato open and investigate the color and texture. Suggest the best cooking method to use on each type. Record your findings in the chart below.

Potato	Skin color	Skin texture	Interior color	Interior texture

2. Choose one type of potato and an appropriate cooking method.
3. Prepare and cook the potatoes. Determine doneness.
4. Have your instructor evaluate the cooked potatoes by completing the Performance Checklist on the next page.

(Continued on next page)

Performance ✔ Checklist

Performance Standards

Level 4—Performs skill without supervision and adapts to problem situations.

Level 3—Performs skill satisfactorily without assistance or supervision.

Level 2—Performs skill satisfactorily, but requires assistance or supervision.

Level 1—Performs parts of skill satisfactorily, but requires considerable assistance or supervision.

Level 0—Cannot perform skill.

Attempt (circle one):   1   2   3   4

Comments: _____

_____

_____

_____

_____

_____

Performance Level Achieved: _____

_____ 1. Follows safety and sanitation practices at all times during this job.

_____ 2. Selects and executes the cooking method correctly.

_____ 3. The potatoes are cooked to the appropriate degree of doneness and held at 140°F or above.

_____ 4. The potatoes retain their shape and have an even, natural color.

_____ 5. The texture of the potatoes is moist, tender, and juicy.

_____ 6. The flavor of the potatoes is characteristic to the type of potatoes.

Instructor's Signature: _____   **Date:** _____

Name _____ Date _____

Preparing Vegetables

Directions: Demonstrate a preparation technique for vegetables by completing the steps that follow.

1. Select one of the following techniques:
   - roasting
   - julienne
   - blanching
   - parboiling
   - shocking
   - washing greens, and cutting vegetables on a mandoline

2. Prepare the Job Plan Sheet on page 168. List each step needed to perform the task. You may use the textbook and any information provided by your instructor.

3. Practice your chosen technique several times. Then prepare a demonstration and show the class how to properly perform your selected technique.

4. Have your instructor evaluate your technique and complete the Performance Checklist.

Performance ✔ Checklist

Performance Standards

Level 4—Performs skill without supervision and adapts to problem situations.

Level 3—Performs skill satisfactorily without assistance or supervision.

Level 2—Performs skill satisfactorily, but requires assistance or supervision.

Level 1—Performs parts of skill satisfactorily, but requires considerable assistance or supervision.

Level 0—Cannot perform skill.

Attempt (circle one):   1   2   3   4

Comments: _____

_____

_____

_____

_____

_____

Performance Level Achieved: _____

_____ 1. Follows safety and sanitation practices at all times during this job.

_____ 2. Executes the preparation technique correctly.

Instructor's Signature: _____ **Date:** _____

(Continued on next page)

Job Plan Sheet

Recipe: _____

Yield: _____   Portion size: _____

Ingredient:	Amount:	Ingredient:	Amount:
_____	_____	_____	_____
_____	_____	_____	_____
_____	_____	_____	_____
_____	_____	_____	_____
_____	_____	_____	_____

Equipment:	Use:	Equipment:	Use:
_____	_____	_____	_____
_____	_____	_____	_____
_____	_____	_____	_____

List each preparation step below.

_____

_____

_____

_____

_____

_____

_____

_____

_____

_____

_____

_____

Vegetable Cookery

Directions: Working in teams, cook vegetables using the appropriate techniques. Complete the steps that follow.

1. Review the rules for cooking red, white, yellow, and green vegetables.
2. Obtain vegetables from your instructor. Select the appropriate cooking method(s) for each type of vegetable.
3. Complete the Job Plan Sheet on page 170 and submit it for instructor approval.
4. Prepare the vegetables according to your approved Job Plan Sheet.
5. Plate and garnish the vegetables appropriately.
6. Have your instructor evaluate your finished product and complete the Performance Checklist.

Performance ✔ Checklist

Performance Standards	Attempt (circle one): 1 2 3 4
Level 4—Performs skill without supervision and adapts to problem situations.	Comments: _____
Level 3—Performs skill satisfactorily without assistance or supervision.	_____
Level 2—Performs skill satisfactorily, but requires assistance or supervision.	_____
Level 1—Performs parts of skill satisfactorily, but requires considerable assistance or supervision.	_____
Level 0—Cannot perform skill.	**Performance Level Achieved:** _____

_____ 1. Follows safety and sanitation practices at all times during this job.

_____ 2. Selects and executes the cooking methods correctly.

_____ 3. Completes the Job Plan Sheet correctly and professionally.

_____ 4. Cooks vegetables to the appropriate degree of doneness following HACCP guidelines.

_____ 5. Cooks vegetables to retain their shape and even, natural color.

_____ 6. Cooks vegetables to proper texture—moist, tender, and juicy.

_____ 7. Prepares vegetables to proper flavor appropriate to type of vegetable.

_____ 8. Plates and garnishes the vegetables artistically.

Instructor's Signature: _____   **Date:** _____

(Continued on next page)

Job Plan Sheet

Recipe: _____

Yield: _____ Portion size: _____

Ingredient:	Amount:	Ingredient:	Amount:
_____	_____	_____	_____
_____	_____	_____	_____
_____	_____	_____	_____
_____	_____	_____	_____
_____	_____	_____	_____

Equipment:	Use:	Equipment:	Use:
_____	_____	_____	_____
_____	_____	_____	_____
_____	_____	_____	_____

List each preparation step below.

_____

_____

_____

_____

_____

_____

_____

_____

_____

_____

_____

_____

Name _____ Date _____   LAB ACTIVITY 95

Scaling Ingredients

Directions: Scale the ingredients provided by your instructor by completing the steps below. Then answer the questions that follow.

Part A
1. Measure the flour, using an 8-oz. volume measuring cup.
2. Weigh the flour on a balance or digital scale.
3. Record the weight in the chart below.
4. Find the difference between the volume and weight. Does the flour weigh 8 oz.? Record the weights in the chart below.
5. Weigh the flour on a portion scale. Record the weight in the chart below.
6. Repeat steps 1–5 for each ingredient listed in the chart below.

Ingredient Measured by Volume	Balance- or Digital-Scale Weight	Portion Scale	Difference Between Volume and Weight
8 oz. Flour			
6 oz. Sugar			
3 oz. Salt			

Part B

1. Was the weight by volume more or less than the balance- or digital-scale weight? Explain why.

_____

_____

2. Was the portion scale weight different than the balance- or digital-scale weight? Explain why.

_____

_____

3. What differences would you see in the finished product if you measured your ingredients by volume instead of weight?

_____

_____

Culinary Essentials Lab Manual
Copyright © Glencoe/McGraw-Hill

171

Converting Yields

Directions: Work in teams. Convert yields by completing the steps that follow.

1. Obtain a formula from your instructor and review it.
2. List each ingredient of your formula in the chart below. Write in the yield.
3. Weigh each ingredient using a balance or digital scale. Record the weight in the chart.
4. Increase the yield by doubling the formula. Write in the new yield in the chart.
5. Find the new weight of each ingredient. Record the weight in the chart.

Ingredient	Original yield	Original weight	New yield	New weight

Bakeshop Ingredients

Directions: In the chart below, describe how each bakeshop ingredient is used.

Ingredient	How it is used
Bread flour	
Cake flour	
Pastry flour	
Water	
Milk and cream	
Vegetable shortening	
Emulsified shortening	
Oil	
Granulated sugar	
Coarse sugar	
Confectioners' sugar	

(Continued on next page)

Ingredient	How it is used
Molasses	
Corn syrup	
Superfine sugar	
Maple syrup	
Honey	
Eggs	
Baking soda	
Baking powder	
Yeast	
Salt	
Spices	
Nuts	
Semisweet chocolate	
Unsweetened chocolate	

The Straight Dough Method

Directions: Work in teams to bake yeast rolls. Complete the steps below.

1. Obtain a yeast roll formula that uses the straight-dough method. Review the formula.

2. Your instructor will assign a roll shape to your team. Review the steps to shaping rolls on pages179-181 of Lab Activity 99. List your procedure below.

_____

_____

_____

_____

_____

_____

_____

_____

_____

_____

_____

_____

_____

_____

_____

_____

3. Use the following formula to convert the yield of your yeast roll formula if needed.

    Step 1   desired yield ÷ existing yield = conversion factor

    Step 2   existing quantity × conversion factor = desired quantity

4. Prepare the yeast rolls. Record the action taken at each step and how long it took in the chart on the next page. By completing the Straight Dough Method Process chart, you can determine how long it takes to make yeast rolls.

(Continued on next page)

Straight-Dough Method Process

Step	Action Taken	Start Time	Stop Time
1. Gathering ingredients			
2. Scaling ingredients			
3. Mixing/kneading			
4. Flour fermentation			
5. Dividing dough			
6. Rounding dough			
7. Bench rest			
8. Shaping dough into roll			
9. Panning dough			
10. Final proof			
11. Baking dough			
12. Cooling rolls			
13. Packaging rolls			

(Continued on next page)

5. Review the duration of each step. In the space provided, list the steps in which you can improve time.

_____

_____

_____

_____

_____

6. Sample your yeast rolls. Then complete the Product Assessment chart below, evaluating the rolls in each category listed. Rate your rolls using the following scale:
1=Poor; **2**=Fair; **3**=Good; **4**=Great.

Product Assessment	
Category	**Results**
Shape	
Crust	
Texture	
Aroma	
Flavor	

(Continued on next page)

7. Present your yeast rolls to your instructor for evaluation and have the Performance Checklist below completed.

Performance ✔ Checklist

Performance Standards
Level 4—Performs skill without supervision and adapts to problem situations.
Level 3—Performs skill satisfactorily without assistance or supervision.
Level 2—Performs skill satisfactorily, but requires assistance or supervision.
Level 1—Performs parts of skill satisfactorily, but requires considerable assistance or supervision.
Level 0—Cannot perform skill.

Attempt (circle one):   1   2   3   4

Comments: _____

_____

_____

_____

_____

_____

Performance Level Achieved: _____

_____ 1. Follows safety and sanitation practices at all times during this job.

_____ 2. Mixes dough to the correct consistency.

_____ 3. Applies the straight-dough method correctly.

_____ 4. Scales ingredients accurately.

_____ 5. Performs mixing/kneading correctly.

_____ 6. Divides dough correctly.

_____ 7. Shapes dough correctly into the assigned roll shape.

_____ 8. Cools dough according to the guidelines in the textbook.

_____ 9. Produces quality bread according to proper flavor, texture, doneness, and appearance.

_____ 10. Wraps and stores the final product safely.

Instructor's Signature: _____ **Date:** _____

Shaping Yeast Rolls

Directions: Work in teams to shape yeast rolls. Complete the steps below.

1. Obtain from your instructor a yeast roll formula that follows the straight-dough method.

2. Review the formula. Use the following formula to convert the yield of your yeast roll formula if needed.

   Step 1   desired yield ÷ existing yield = conversion factor

   Step 2   existing quantity × conversion factor = desired quantity

3. Prepare the dough following the steps outlined in the straight-dough method until you reach the step on shaping dough.

4. Using a dough scraper or bench knife, scale the dough into four equal portions. Weigh each portion to ensure they are the same size.

5. Shape each scaled portion of dough into the types of rolls listed below. Refer to the instructions and diagrams that follow.

   A. Braided loaves
   B. Parker house rolls

   C. Cloverleaf rolls
   D. Single-knotted rolls

Braided Loaves

1. Divide the scaled dough into three equal portions as shown.

2. Place the pieces of dough on the pre-floured bench.

3. Using the palm of your hand, roll the dough into long, narrow ropes, as shown.

4. Cross the bottom end of the rope over the middle of the rope as shown.

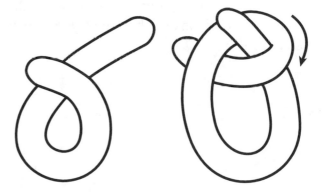

(Continued on next page)

5. Pull the top end of the rope through the loop as shown.

6. Twist the dough at the loop, forming a figure eight as shown.

7. Pull the loose end of the rope through the newly formed loop (the bottom part of the figure eight) as shown.

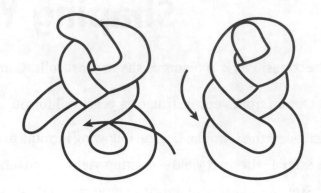

Parker House Rolls

1. Divide the scaled dough into three equal portions.

2. Round the dough as shown.

3. Place the ball of dough on the pre-floured bench.

4. Using a rolling pin, flatten only the center of the dough as shown.

5. Fold the flattened dough in half as shown.

6. Using the palm of your hand, press on the folded edge of the dough to make a crease as shown.

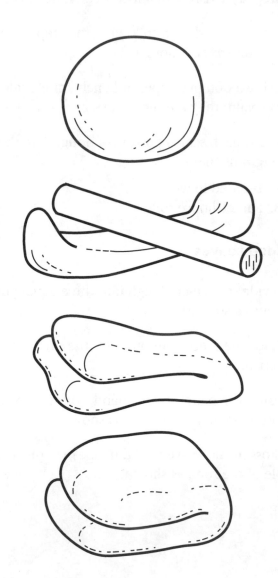

(Continued on next page)

Culinary Essentials Lab Manual
Copyright © Glencoe/McGraw-Hill

Cloverleaf Rolls

1. Divide the scaled dough into smaller parts.

2. Then divide the smaller pieces of dough into three equal parts as shown.

3. Shape the three equal parts into balls as shown.

4. Place three balls in each greased muffin tin as shown.

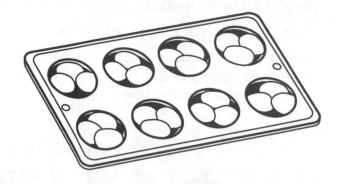

Single-Knotted Rolls

1. Divide the scaled dough into three equal parts.

2. Place the dough on the pre-floured bench.

3. Using the palm of your hand, roll the dough into long, narrow ropes as shown.

4. Cross the bottom end of the rope over the top end of the rope as shown.

5. Tuck the end in the loop as shown.

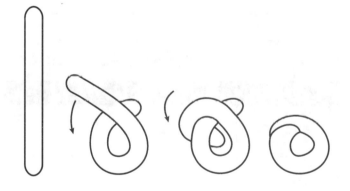

(Continued on next page)

6. After the rolls are shaped, complete the steps of the straight-dough method.

7. Bake your rolls following your formula.

8. Sample your yeast rolls. Then complete the Product Assessment charts that follow, evaluating the rolls in each category listed. Rate your rolls using the following scale:
1=Poor; 2=Fair; 3=Good; 4=Great.

| Product Assessment: Braided Loaves ||
Category	Results
Shape	
Crust	
Texture	
Aroma	
Flavor	

| Product Assessment: Parker House Rolls ||
Category	Results
Shape	
Crust	
Texture	
Aroma	
Flavor	

(Continued on next page)

Culinary Essentials Lab Manual
Copyright © Glencoe/McGraw-Hill

Product Assessment: Cloverleaf Rolls

Category	Results
Shape	
Crust	
Texture	
Aroma	
Flavor	

Product Assessment: Single-Knotted Rolls

Category	Results
Shape	
Crust	
Texture	
Aroma	
Flavor	

(Continued on next page)

9. Present your yeast rolls to your instructor for evaluation and have the Performance Checklist below completed.

Performance ✔ Checklist

Performance Standards

Level 4—Performs skill without supervision and adapts to problem situations.

Level 3—Performs skill satisfactorily without assistance or supervision.

Level 2—Performs skill satisfactorily, but requires assistance or supervision.

Level 1—Performs parts of skill satisfactorily, but requires considerable assistance or supervision.

Level 0—Cannot perform skill.

Attempt (circle one): 1 2 3 4

Comments: _____

_____

_____

_____

_____

_____

Performance Level Achieved: _____

_____ 1. Follows safety and sanitation practices at all times during this job.

_____ 2. Mixes the dough to the correct consistency.

_____ 3. Applies the straight-dough method correctly.

_____ 4. Scales the dough into four portions correctly.

_____ 5. Shapes the braided loaves correctly, and the final product resembled braided loaves.

_____ 6. Shapes the Parker House rolls correctly, and the final product resembled Parker House rolls.

_____ 7. Shapes the cloverleaf rolls correctly, and the final product resembled cloverleaf rolls.

_____ 8. Shapes the single-knotted rolls correctly, and the final product resembled single-knotted rolls.

_____ 9. Produces a product that displays quality characteristics for flavor, texture, doneness, and appearance.

_____ 10. Wraps and stores the final product safely.

Instructor's Signature: _____ **Date:** _____

The Biscuit Method

Directions: Prepare biscuits using the biscuit method. Complete the steps that follow.

1. Obtain a biscuit formula. Review the formula.
2. Convert the yield of the formula if necessary using the following formula:

   Step 1 desired yield ÷ existing yield = conversion factor

   Step 2 existing quantity × conversion factor = desired quantity
3. Complete the Job Plan Sheet below. Submit it to your instructor for approval.

Job Plan Sheet

Recipe: _____

Yield: _____   **Portion size:** _____

Ingredient:	Amount:	Ingredient:	Amount:
_____	_____	_____	_____
_____	_____	_____	_____
_____	_____	_____	_____
_____	_____	_____	_____
_____	_____	_____	_____

Equipment:	Use:	Equipment:	Use:
_____	_____	_____	_____
_____	_____	_____	_____
_____	_____	_____	_____

List each step in the preparation process:

_____

_____

_____

_____

(Continued on next page)

4. Make biscuits following your formula and approved Job Plan Sheet. Record the action taken at each step and how long it took in the chart below.

The Biscuit Method Process

Step	Action Taken	Start Time	Stop Time
1. Gathering the ingredients			
2. Preparing the pan			
3. Scaling the ingredients			
4. Sifting the dry ingredients			
5. Cutting in the shortening			
6. Preparing the liquid ingredients			
7. Combining the liquid and dry ingredients			
8. Flouring the dough			
9. Kneading the dough			
10. Resting the dough			
11. Rolling the dough			
12. Shaping the dough			
13. Baking the dough			

(Continued on next page)

5. Review the duration of each step listed in the chart on the previous page. In the space provided, list the steps in which you can improve time.

_____

_____

_____

_____

_____

6. Sample your biscuits. Then complete the Product Assessment chart below, evaluating the final product in each category listed. Rate your biscuits using the following scale:
   1–Poor; **2**–Fair; **3**–Good; **4**–Great.

Product Assessment	
Category	**Results**
Shape	
Crust	
Texture	
Aroma	
Flavor	

7. Present your biscuits to your instructor for evaluation and have your instructor complete the Performance Checklist on page 188.

(Continued on next page)

Performance ✔ Checklist

Performance Standards

Level 4—Performs skill without supervision and adapts to problem situations.

Level 3—Performs skill satisfactorily without assistance or supervision.

Level 2—Performs skill satisfactorily, but requires assistance or supervision.

Level 1—Performs parts of skill satisfactorily, but requires considerable assistance or supervision.

Level 0—Cannot perform skill.

Attempt (circle one): 1   2   3   4

Comments: _____

_____

_____

_____

_____

_____

Performance Level Achieved: _____

_____ 1. Follows safety and sanitation practices at all times during this job.

_____ 2. Prepares the Job Plan Sheet correctly and professionally.

_____ 3. Follows the Job Plan Sheet during preparation and baking.

_____ 4. Executes the biscuit method correctly.

_____ 5. Prepares the sheet pan correctly.

_____ 6. Sifts the dry ingredients before combining them.

_____ 7. Cuts the shortening into the dry ingredients at the correct time in the process.

_____ 8. Whisks the eggs and milk together in a separate stainless steel bowl.

_____ 9. Mixes the liquid and dry ingredients lightly.

_____ 10. Performs the kneading process correctly.

_____ 11. Lets the dough rest for 15 minutes before shaping and baking.

_____ 12. Prepares biscuits that display quality characteristics for proper flavor, texture, doneness, and appearance.

Instructor's Signature: _____ **Date:** _____

The Blending Method

Directions: Prepare a quick bread product using the blending method. Complete the steps below.

1. Obtain a quick bread formula for a loaf bread. Review the formula.
2. Convert the yield of the formula if necessary using the following conversion formula:
   Step 1   desired yield ÷ existing yield = conversion factor
   Step 2   existing quantity × conversion factor = desired quantity
3. Create a Job Plan Sheet on a separate sheet of paper.
4. Make your quick bread product following your formula and approved Job Plan Sheet. Record the action taken at each step and how long it took in the chart below.

Blending-Method Process			
Step	**Action Taken**	**Start Time**	**Stop Time**
1. Gathering ingredients			
2. Greasing deep pans			
3. Scaling ingredients			
4. Combining liquid ingredients			
5. Sifting ingredients			
6. Combining liquid and dry ingredients			
7. Mixing the batter			
8. Scaling the batter			
9. Baking the batter			
10. Cooling the loaf bread			
11. Storing the loaf bread			

(Continued on next page)

5. Sample your finished product. Then complete the Product Assessment chart below, evaluating the final product in each category listed. Rate your product using the following scale:
1=Poor; 2=Fair; 3=Good; 4=Great.
Share your results with the class.

Product Assessment

Category	Results
Shape	
Crust	
Texture	
Aroma	
Flavor	

6. Present your final product to your instructor for evaluation and have the Performance Checklist below completed.

Performance ✔ Checklist

Performance Standards

Level 4—Performs skill without supervision and adapts to problem situations.

Level 3—Performs skill satisfactorily without assistance or supervision.

Level 2—Performs skill satisfactorily, but requires assistance or supervision.

Level 1—Performs parts of skill satisfactorily, but requires considerable assistance or supervision.

Level 0—Cannot perform skill.

Attempt (circle one): 1 2 3 4

Comments: _____

_____

_____

_____

_____

_____

Performance Level Achieved: _____

_____ 1. Follows safety and sanitation practices at all times during this job.

_____ 2. Executes the blending method correctly.

_____ 3. Produces a baked product that displays quality characteristics for flavor, texture, doneness, and appearance.

Instructor's Signature: _____ **Date:** _____

The Creaming Method

Directions: Make a quick bread product using the creaming method. Complete the steps below.

1. Obtain a quick bread formula that uses the creaming method. Review the formula.
2. Convert the yield of the formula if necessary using the following conversion formula:
   Step 1   desired yield ÷ existing yield = conversion factor
   Step 2   existing quantity × conversion factor = desired quantity
3. Create a Job Plan Sheet on a separate sheet of paper.
4. Make your quick bread product following your formula and approved Job Plan Sheet. Record the action taken at each step and how long it took in the chart below.

Creaming Method Process			
Step	**Action Taken**	**Start Time**	**Stop Time**
1. Gathering ingredients			
2. Greasing the pan			
3. Scaling ingredients			
4. Sifting the dry ingredients			
5. Combining solid fat and sugar			
6. Adding eggs			
7. Adding flour and liquid ingredients			
8. Portioning batter			
9. Baking batter			
10. Cooling baked product			
11. Storing baked product			

(Continued on next page)

5. Sample your finished product. Then complete the Product Assessment chart, evaluating the final product in each category listed. Rate your finished product using the following scale:
1=Poor; **2**=Fair; **3**=Good; **4**=Great.
Share your results with the class.

Product Assessment	
Category	**Results**
Shape	
Crust	
Texture	
Aroma	
Flavor	

6. Present your final product to your instructor for evaluation and have the Performance Checklist below completed.

Performance ✔ Checklist

Performance Standards

Level 4—Performs skill without supervision and adapts to problem situations.

Level 3—Performs skill satisfactorily without assistance or supervision.

Level 2—Performs skill satisfactorily, but requires assistance or supervision.

Level 1—Performs parts of skill satisfactorily, but requires considerable assistance or supervision.

Level 0—Cannot perform skill.

Attempt (circle one):   1   2   3   4

Comments: _____

_____

_____

_____

_____

_____

Performance Level Achieved: _____

_____ 1. Follows safety and sanitation practices at all times during this job.

_____ 2. Prepares and follows the Job Plan Sheet correctly and professionally.

_____ 3. Executes the creaming method correctly.

_____ 4. Produces a baked product that displays quality characteristics for flavor, texture, doneness, and appearance.

Instructor's Signature: _____   **Date:** _____

Culinary Essentials Lab Manual
Copyright © Glencoe/McGraw-Hill

Banana Nut Bread Production

Directions: Working in teams, prepare banana nut bread by using the recipe below. With your instructor, rate the finished nut bread for proper flavor, texture, and appearance:

1=Poor; 2=Fair; 3=Good; 4=Great.

PASTRY TECHNIQUE:
Blending

Blending:
1. Combine the dry ingredients on low speed.
2. Add the softened fat(s) and liquid(s).
3. Mix the ingredients on low speed.
4. Increase the speed gradually.

HAZARDOUS FOOD:
Eggs

NUTRITION:
Calories: 201
Fat: 6.5 g
Protein: 2.95 g

Banana Nut Bread

YIELD: 6 LBS., 3⅝ OZ.   SERVING SIZE: 3 OZ.

INGREDIENTS:

1 lb., 4 oz.	Sugar, granulated
6 oz.	High-ratio shortening
½ oz.	Baking soda, sifted
½ oz.	Lemon powder
⅛ oz.	Salt
8 oz.	Bananas, fresh or canned, mashed
2 oz.	Eggs, whole
1 lb., 8 oz.	Water, cold
1 lb.	Bread flour, sifted
1 lb.	Cake flour, sifted
½ oz.	Baking powder, sifted
4 oz.	Nuts, finely chopped
2 oz.	Banana compound

METHOD OF PREPARATION:

1. Gather the equipment and ingredients.
2. Place the granulated sugar, shortening, baking soda, lemon powder, and salt in a mixing bowl with paddle attachment; cream for 2 minutes.
3. Add the bananas and eggs to the mixture in the bowl; cream for an additional 1 minute.
4. Add one-third of the amount of the water and mix at low speed.
5. Sift together the flours and baking powder.
6. Add the sifted ingredients to the mixture in two stages. Mix at low speed.
7. Add one-third of the water, and mix only until all ingredients are incorporated. Do not overmix.
8. Scrape the bowl well.
9. Add the chopped nuts and banana compound.
10. Add the remaining water; mix well.
11. Scale evenly into 5 loaf pans, 19 oz. per pan.
12. Bake at 375°F until the loaves are light brown overall and firm in the center.
13. Cool. Then remove from the pans.

Making Pancakes with Maple Syrup

Directions: Working in teams, prepare pancakes by using the recipe below. With your instructor, rate the finished product for proper flavor, texture, and appearance:

1=Poor; **2**=Fair; **3**=Good; **4**=Great.

COOKING TECHNIQUE:
Bake

Bake:
1. Preheat the oven.
2. Place the food product on the appropriate rack.

HACCP:

Hold at 140°F or above.
Hold unused batter at 41°F or below.

HAZARDOUS FOODS:
Milk
Pasteurized eggs

NUTRITION:
Calories: 478
Fat: 11.6 g
Protein: 9.63 g

CHEF NOTE:
For best results, make pancakes to order.

Pancakes with Maple Syrup

YIELD: 50 SERVINGS   SERVING SIZE: 4 EACH

INGREDIENTS:

1 qt.	Pasteurized eggs
3 qts.	Milk
2 tbsp.	Vanilla extract
6 lbs.	All-purpose flour
8 oz.	Sugar
6 oz.	Baking powder
1 lb.	Butter, melted
2 qts.	Maple syrup, heated and kept warm at 140°F

METHOD OF PREPARATION:

1. Preheat the griddle.
2. In a mixing bowl, beat the eggs.
3. Add the milk and vanilla to the beaten eggs, and mix well. Set aside.
4. Mix all of the dry ingredients together. Add the egg mixture, and whisk to a smooth batter.
5. Stir the butter into the mixture.
6. Let the batter rest for 1 hour before using.
7. To cook, pour approximately 2 oz. of batter on a seasoned, lightly buttered griddle.
8. Cook until the bubbles appear on the top and the edges become dry.
9. Turn over, and bake the other side until done. Serve immediately, or hold at 140°F or above.
10. Hold the unused batter at 41°F or below if not used immediately.
11. Serve with warm syrup.
12. Repeat the procedure until all of the batter is used.

Pancake & Waffle Production

Directions: Prepare pancakes and waffles from the same formula. Complete the steps below.

1. Obtain a pancake and a waffle formula from your instructor. Review each formula and compare the ingredients.

2. Complete the Quick Bread Ingredients worksheet below by writing in the correct proportion of each ingredient. Indicate which leavening agent you are using and whether any seasonings or flavorings were added.

Quick Bread Ingredients		
Ingredient	**Amount for Pancakes**	**Amount for Waffles**
Flour		
Eggs		
Fat		
Sugar		
Salt		
Leavening agent		
Liquid		
Other		

3. List your procedure for each product on a separate sheet of paper.

4. Create a Job Plan Sheet on a separate sheet of paper.

5. Prepare your pancake and waffle products.

6. Sample each of your finished products. Then complete the Product Assessment chart that follows, evaluating the final products in each category listed. Rate your pancakes and waffles using the following rating scale:
   1=Poor; **2**=Fair; **3**=Good; **4**=Great.
   Share your results with the class.

7. Have your instructor complete the Performance Checklist on the next page.

(Continued on next page)

Product Assessment

Category	Pancake Results	Waffle Results
Shape		
Crust		
Texture		
Aroma		
Flavor		

Performance ✔ Checklist

Performance Standards

Level 4—Performs skill without supervision and adapts to problem situations.

Level 3—Performs skill satisfactorily without assistance or supervision.

Level 2—Performs skill satisfactorily, but requires assistance or supervision.

Level 1—Performs parts of skill satisfactorily, but requires considerable assistance or supervision.

Level 0—Cannot perform skill.

Attempt (circle one):   1   2   3   4

Comments: _____

_____

_____

_____

_____

_____

Performance Level Achieved: _____

_____ 1. Follows safety and sanitation practices at all times during this job.

_____ 2. Measures quick bread ingredients accurately.

_____ 3. Uses the correct quick bread mixing method for each product.

_____ 4. Carefully times mixing so that the batter was not over- or undermixed.

_____ 5. Produces pancakes and waffles that display quality characteristics for proper flavor, texture, doneness, and appearance.

Instructor's Signature: _____ **Date:** _____

Cookie Production

Directions: Working in teams, scale, mix, and bake different types of cookies.

1. Prepare three dozen of each of the following types of cookies. Obtain cookie formulas from your instructor. Then review the formulas.
   Team A: Drop cookies   **Team C:** Molded cookies
   Team B: Rolled cookies   **Team D:** Bar cookies
2. Make your cookies following your formulas. Convert the yield of the formulas as necessary using the following conversion formula:
   Step 1   desired yield ÷ existing yield = conversion factor
   Step 2   existing quantity × conversion factor = desired quantity
3. Make your cookies following your formulas. Record the action taken at each step in the chart below. Be sure to indicate your stop and start times for each ingredient.

Step	Action Taken	Start Time	Stop Time
1. Gathering ingredients			
2. Greasing the pan			
3. Scaling ingredients			
4. Sifting the dry ingredients			
5. Combining solid fat and sugar			
6. Adding eggs			
7. Adding flour and liquid ingredients			
8. Portioning batter			
9. Baking batter			
10. Cooling baked product			

4. Review the duration of each step in your formulas. On a separate sheet of paper, list the steps in which you can improve time.

(Continued on next page)

5. Sample your cookies. Then complete the Product Assessment chart below, evaluating the final products in each category listed. Rate your cookies using the following scale:
   1=Poor; **2**=Fair; **3**=Good; **4**=Great.
   Share your results with the class.

Cookie Type: _____

Product Assessment	
Category	**Results**
Shape	
Crust	
Texture	
Aroma	
Flavor	

6. Present your cookies to your instructor for evaluation, and have the Performance Checklist on the next page completed.

Performance ✔ Checklist

Performance Standards
Level 4—Performs skill without supervision and adapts to problem situations.
Level 3—Performs skill satisfactorily without assistance or supervision.
Level 2—Performs skill satisfactorily, but requires assistance or supervision.
Level 1—Performs parts of skill satisfactorily, but requires considerable assistance or supervision.
Level 0—Cannot perform skill.

Attempt (circle one): 1 2 3 4

Comments: _____

_____

_____

_____

_____

_____

Performance Level Achieved: _____

_____ 1. Follows safety and sanitation practices at all times during this job.

_____ 2. Accurately scales and mixes ingredients following formula directions.

_____ 3. Correctly divides and bakes cookie batter for all formulas as directed.

_____ 4. Produces cookies that display proper quality characteristics for flavor, texture, doneness, and appearance.

Instructor's Signature: _____ **Date:** _____

Cake Production

Directions: Work in teams to prepare cakes. Then create icing and finish the cake for evaluation. Sell your cakes in the school restaurant, either whole or by the piece.

1. Divide into five teams. Each team will prepare their assigned cake. Obtain a cake formula from your instructor. Review the formula and the blending method.

   Team A: Pound cake   **Team D:** Chiffon cake

   Team B: Sponge or foam cake   **Team E:** High-ratio cake

   Team C: Angel food cake

2. Prepare your team's cake as directed in the formula. Use the following formula to convert the yield of the recipe if needed. Create a Job Plan Sheet on a separate sheet of paper.

   Step 1   desired yield ÷ existing yield = conversion factor

   Step 2   existing quantity × conversion factor = desired quantity

3. In the chart below, list the steps taken to make your assigned cake type, the actions taken at each step, and the start and stop times of each step.

Type of Cake: _____   Mixing Method: _____

Step	Action Taken	Start Time	Stop Time
1.			
2.			
3.			
4.			
5.			
6.			
7.			
8.			
9.			

(Continued on next page)

4. Bake your cake as directed in your formula. Test your cake for doneness.

5. Select and obtain an icing formula for your cake.

6. List the steps for preparing the icing and the action taken at each step in the chart that follows. Include your start and stop times for each step.

Type of Icing: _____

Step	Action Taken	Start Time	Stop Time
1.			
2.			
3.			
4.			
5.			
6.			
7.			
8.			
9.			

7. Apply the icing to your cake as directed.

8. Taste and evaluate your cake. Rate your cake using the following scale:
   1=Poor; **2**=Fair; **3**=Good; **4**=Great.
   Record your ratings in the Product Assessment chart on the next page. Share your results with the class.

(Continued on next page)

Product Assessment

Category	Results
Shape	
Crust	
Texture	
Aroma	
Flavor	

9. Have your instructor evaluate your cake using the Performance Checklist that follows.

Performance ✔ Checklist

Performance Standards

Level 4—Performs skill without supervision and adapts to problem situations.

Level 3—Performs skill satisfactorily without assistance or supervision.

Level 2—Performs skill satisfactorily, but requires assistance or supervision.

Level 1—Performs parts of skill satisfactorily, but requires considerable assistance or supervision.

Level 0—Cannot perform skill.

Attempt (circle one):   1   2   3   4

Comments: _____

_____

_____

_____

_____

_____

Performance Level Achieved: _____

_____ 1. Follows safety and sanitation practices at all times during this job.

_____ 2. Mixes the cake ingredients properly, resulting in a quality product.

_____ 3. Uses the correct steps and actions in the blending method to create cakes.

_____ 4. Scales the batter correctly into prepared pans for even baking.

_____ 5. Selects the appropriate icing for the cakes.

_____ 6. Produces icing of the right consistency.

_____ 7. Produces cakes that display quality characteristics for proper flavor, texture, doneness, and appearance.

Instructor's Signature: _____ **Date:** _____

Vanilla Chiffon Genoise Production

Directions: Working in teams, prepare the Vanilla Chiffon Genoise by following the recipe below. With your instructor, rate the finished product for proper flavor, texture, and appearance:

1=Poor; 2=Fair; 3=Good; 4=Great.

PASTRY TECHNIQUES:
Whipping, Combining

Whipping:
1. Hold the whip at a 45° angle.
2. Create circles, using a circular motion.
3. The circular motion needs to be perpendicular to the bowl.

Combining:
Bringing together two or more components.
1. Prepare the components to be combined.
2. Add one to the other, using the appropriate mixing method (if needed).

HAZARDOUS FOODS:
Egg yolks
Egg whites

NUTRITION:
Calories: 225
Protein: 4.74 g
Fat: 8.99 g

Vanilla Chiffon Genoise

YIELD: 10 LBS., 6 OZ. (SEVEN, 9-IN. CAKES)   SERVINGS: 70

INGREDIENTS:

2 lbs.	Egg yolks
3 lbs.	Sugar, granulated
12 oz.	Oil, vegetable
2 lbs.	Egg whites
2 lbs., 4 oz.	Flour, cake, sifted
1 oz.	Baking powder
5 oz.	Water, room temperature
To taste	Extract, vanilla

METHOD OF PREPARATION:

1. Gather the equipment and scale the ingredients.
2. Properly grease the cake pans.
3. Place the egg yolks and half of the granulated sugar in a 5-qt. mixing bowl; whip to full volume.
4. Continue mixing on medium speed, and slowly incorporate the oil.
5. In another 5-qt. mixing bowl, whip the egg whites to a medium peak; slowly add the remaining granulated sugar to make a meringue.
6. Sift together the cake flour and baking powder.
7. Combine the water and vanilla extract.
8. Alternately add the flour and water mixtures into the yolk mixture by hand.
9. Fold the meringue into the batter.
10. Scale 1 lb., 8 oz. batter into each greased, paper-lined 9-in. cake pan.
11. Bake at 360°F until spongy in the center.

Pie Production

Directions: Work in teams to prepare pies. Sell your pies in the school restaurant, either whole or by the piece.

1. Divide into four teams. Each team will prepare three of their assigned type of pie. Obtain your pie formula from your instructor. Review the formula. Create a Job Plan Sheet on a separate sheet of paper.

   Team A: Apple pie (double crust)   **Team C:** Chocolate pie (single crust)

   Team B: Cherry pie (double crust)   **Team D:** Coconut cream pie (single crust)

   Prepare your crusts from scratch, but use premade fillings for your assigned type of pie.

2. Prepare your team's pies as directed in the formula. Use the following formula to convert the yield of the recipe if needed.

   Step 1   desired yield ÷ existing yield = conversion factor

   Step 2   existing quantity × conversion factor = desired quantity

3. In the chart below, list the steps taken to make your assigned pies, the action taken at each step, and the start and stop times of each step.

Type of Pie: _____

Step	Action Taken	Start Time	Stop Time
1.			
2.			
3.			
4.			
5.			
6.			
7.			
8.			

(Continued on next page)

4. Bake your pies as directed in your formula. Test your pies for doneness.
5. Taste and evaluate your pies. Rate your pies using the following scale:
   1=Poor; **2**=Fair; **3**=Good; **4**=Great.
   Record your ratings in the Product Assessment chart below. Share your results with the class.

Product Assessment	
Category	**Results**
Shape	
Crust	
Texture	
Aroma	
Flavor	

6. Have your instructor evaluate your pie using the Performance Checklist that follows.

Performance ✔ Checklist

Performance Standards

Level 4—Performs skill without supervision and adapts to problem situations.

Level 3—Performs skill satisfactorily without assistance or supervision.

Level 2—Performs skill satisfactorily, but requires assistance or supervision.

Level 1—Performs parts of skill satisfactorily, but requires considerable assistance or supervision.

Level 0—Cannot perform skill.

Attempt (circle one): 1 2 3 4

Comments: _____

_____

_____

_____

_____

_____

Performance Level Achieved: _____

_____ 1. Follows safety and sanitation practices at all times during this job.

_____ 2. Mixes the pie ingredients properly, resulting in a quality product.

_____ 3. Takes the correct steps and actions to create the pies.

_____ 4. Scales the dough correctly.

_____ 5. Pans the dough correctly.

_____ 6. Produces pies that display quality characteristics for proper flavor, texture, doneness, and appearance.

Instructor's Signature: _____ **Date:** _____

Pie Dough Production

Directions: Working in teams, prepare basic pie dough by following the recipe below. Use the pie dough to prepare the pie(s) of your choice. With your instructor, rate the finished product for proper flavor, texture, and appearance:

1=Poor; **2**=Fair; **3**=Good; **4**=Great.

PASTRY TECHNIQUE:
Combining

Combining:
Bringing together two or more components.
1. Prepare the components to be combined.
2. Add one to the other, using the appropriate mixing method (if needed).

NUTRITION:
Calories: 135
Protein: 1.83 g
Fat: 9.69 g

CHEF NOTES:
1. The dry milk solids and the sugar can be sifted at the beginning with the pastry flour. The process would be continued in the same manner.
2. Basic pie dough can be used for many applications. The nutrition analysis is based on 1 oz. of dough.

Basic Pie Dough

YIELD: 1 LB., 8-¼ OZ. (THREE, 8-OZ. CRUSTS)   SERVING SIZE: 1 OZ.

INGREDIENTS:	
12 oz.	Flour, pastry
8 oz.	Shortening, vegetable
¼ oz.	Salt
4 oz.	Water, ice-cold
0–1 oz.	Dried milk solids (optional)

METHOD OF PREPARATION:

1. Gather the equipment and scale the ingredients.

2. Sift the flour to aerate it; removing lumps and impurities.

3. Cut the shortening, by hand, into the flour.

4. Dissolve the salt in the cold water.

5. Incorporate the water into the flour until it is sticky. Do not over-work the dough.

6. Allow the dough to rest and chill properly, preferably overnight.

7. Divide the dough into 3, 8–oz. portions.

8. Roll out the dough on a lightly floured pastry cloth. Roll the dough to about a ⅛–in. thickness in a circular form. The dough should be about 1–in. larger than the inverted pie pan.

9. Fold the rolled-out dough in half and carefully place the dough over half the pie pan. Unfold the dough to cover the entire rim of the pie pan. Gently pat the dough from the center of the pan out to work out any air bubbles under the crust.

Cream Puff Production

Directions: Working in teams, prepare cream puffs by following the recipe below. With your instructor, rate the finished product for proper flavor, texture, and appearance:

1=Poor; **2**=Fair; **3**=Good; **4**=Great.

Basic Cream Puffs

YIELD: 25 CREAM PUFFS   SERVING SIZE: 2 OZ.

INGREDIENTS:

8 oz.	Unsalted butter or shortening
¼ oz.	Salt
¼ oz.	Granulated sugar
1 lb.	Water or whole milk
10½ oz.	Sifted bread flour
1 lb.	Eggs

METHOD OF PREPARATION:

1. Gather the equipment and ingredients.
2. Place the butter, salt, granulated sugar, and water or milk in a medium pot.
3. Bring to a boil.
4. Add all of the sifted flour at once.
5. Stir with a wooden spoon for approximately 5 minutes or until the mixture forms a ball that does not stick to the inside of the pot.
6. Cook at this point for an additional 3 minutes.
7. Remove from the heat, and place the mixture in a mixing bowl.
8. Mix on low speed until cooled slightly.
9. Add the eggs gradually; mix at low speed; make sure the eggs are fully incorporated before the next addition.
10. When the eggs are fully incorporated, use a pastry bag and tip to pipe the mixture into the desired shapes on parchment-lined sheet pans. Makes about 25, 2-oz. cream puffs.
11. Bake at 400°F–425°F until brown and dry on the inside, or about 20 minutes.
12. Fill with prepared pastry cream and serve.

PASTRY TECHNIQUES:
Boiling, Combining, Piping

Boiling:
1. Bring the cooking liquid to a rapid boil.
2. Stir the contents.

Combining:
Bringing together 2 or more components.
1. Prepare the components to be combined.
2. Add one to the other, using the appropriate mixing method.

Piping:
With bag:
1. Use a disposable bag with a tip to the appropriate size.
2. Fill to no more that half full.
3. Burp the bag.
With cone:
1. Cut and fold the piping cone to the appropriate size.
2. Fill the cone with a small amount.
3. Fold the ends to form a triangle.
4. Pipe the desired designs.

HAZARDOUS FOODS:
Milk
Eggs

NUTRITION:
Calories: 136
Fat: 9.37 g
Protein: 3.8 g

Specialty Dessert Production

Directions: Work in teams to prepare specialty desserts. Sell your desserts in the school restaurant, either whole or by the serving.

1. Divide into four teams. Each team will prepare three of their assigned type of specialty dessert. Obtain your specialty dessert formula from your instructor. Review the formula. Create a Job Plan Sheet on a separate sheet of paper.
   Team A: Pudding (chocolate or vanilla)   **Team C:** Mousse
   Team B: Baked custard   **Team D:** Molded gelatin
2. Prepare 10 servings of your team's assigned specialty dessert. Use the following formula to convert the yield of the recipe if needed.
   Step 1   desired yield ÷ existing yield = conversion factor
   Step 2   existing quantity × conversion factor = desired quantity
3. In the chart below, list the steps taken to make your assigned specialty dessert, the action taken at each step, and the start and stop times of each step.

Type of Specialty Dessert: _____

Step	Action Taken	Start Time	Stop Time
1.			
2.			
3.			
4.			
5.			
6.			
7.			
8.			

(Continued on next page)

4. Make your specialty dessert as directed in your formula.
5. Taste and evaluate your dessert. Rate your dessert using the following scale:
   1=Poor; **2**=Fair; **3**=Good; **4**=Great.
   Record your ratings in the Product Assessment chart below. Share your results with the class.

Product Assessment	
Category	**Results**
Shape	
Crust	
Texture	
Aroma	
Flavor	

6. Have your instructor evaluate your dessert using the Performance Checklist that follows.

Performance ✔ Checklist

Performance Standards

Level 4—Performs skill without supervision and adapts to problem situations.

Level 3—Performs skill satisfactorily without assistance or supervision.

Level 2—Performs skill satisfactorily, but requires assistance or supervision.

Level 1—Performs parts of skill satisfactorily, but requires considerable assistance or supervision.

Level 0—Cannot perform skill.

Attempt (circle one): 1 2 3 4

Comments: _____

_____

_____

_____

_____

_____

Performance Level Achieved: _____

_____ 1. Follows safety and sanitation practices at all times during this job.

_____ 2. Mixes the dessert ingredients properly, resulting in a quality product.

_____ 3. Takes the correct steps and actions to create the dessert.

_____ 4. Prepares a dessert that displays quality characteristics for proper flavor, texture, temperature, and appearance.

Instructor's Signature: _____ **Date:** _____